CHINA TOWN KITCHEN

CHINA TOWN KITCHEN

From Noodles to Nuoc Cham

Delicious Dishes from Southeast Asian Ingredients

LIZZIE MABBOTT

An Hachette UK Company
www.hachette.co.uk

First published in Great Britain in 2015 by
Mitchell Beazley, a division of Octopus Publishing Group Ltd.
Endeavour House, 189 Shaftesbury Avenue, London WC2H 8JY
www.octopusbooks.co.uk
www.octopusbooksusa.com

Distributed in the US by Hachette Book Group
1290 Avenue of the Americas, 4th and 5th Floors
New York, NY 10020

Distributed in Canada by Canadian Manda Group
664 Annette St.,Toronto, Ontario, Canada M6S 2C8

ISBN 978 1 78472 031 5
A CIP catalog record for this book is available from the British Library.

Printed and bound in China
10 9 8 7 6 5 4 3 2 1

Publishing Director Stephanie Jackson
Senior Editor Sybella Stephens
Copy Editor Jo Richardson
Deputy Art Director & Designer Yasia Williams-Leedham
Illustrator Abigail Read
Photographer David Munns
Prop Stylist & Art Director Tabitha Hawkins
Home Economist Annie Rigg
Senior Production Manager Peter Hunt

CONTENTS

INTRODUCTION

Of half Chinese and half English parentage, I grew up in Hong Kong. It's a smelly, noisy, and hectic city; the name translates rather romantically as "fragrant harbor"— really, it is anything but. Most people who visit are completely overwhelmed by it. My childhood memories are tinged with the smell of food cooking street-side, mingled with traffic fumes and garbage. Add to this heady mix the whiff of gasoline from the sampans and ferries gathering in said harbor, and they blend together to make an unforgettable atmosphere. In summer, the temperatures reach a high of 95°F with humidity only known in subtropical countries; when visiting recently, as my hair turned into a bird's nest, I wondered how I coped. I imagine I was less concerned about how I looked back then.

Growing up, some of my peers lived a more sterile life in townhouses in exclusive areas, their parents being expats sent by their employers with expense accounts to pay the sky-high rents. When visiting, I was fascinated by the stairs they actually had in their houses. We were the opposite; my father moved to Hong Kong in the early 80s on a whim and my mother was a local. We lived just about everywhere on Hong Kong Island—from a relaxed, beachside apartment in the touristy Stanley area, to high-rise housing projects in Aberdeen and, most memorably, the grimy confines of Causeway Bay. My daily trip to school involved negotiating the dank, dark corridors of our apartment building, lit by flickering fluorescent lights, and then waiting at the bus stop early in the morning while butchers ferried carcasses down the streets, wearing them like a grotesque piggyback.

Although Hong Kong was a bustling place, it was safe on the streets and from a young age I was given absolute freedom of it. Outdoors in the stifling heat just off the busy roads, men and young students alike would sit on plastic chairs slurping up noodles, steam rising to their faces. Vendors sold fishballs on sticks, the charcoal enticing you in, finishing them with a lick of curry sauce and a shake of chili powder while you impatiently waited for them to get cool enough to eat. We would spend weekends getting on the ferry to Lamma Island to gorge on seafood, and I would pretend to be the hand of God as I gleefully picked out a doomed fish from the tank to be freshly dispatched for our lunch. My favorite dish was clams freshly stir-fried with black beans, garlic, and chile. I'd suck the flesh out of one half of the shells, sauce dribbling down my face and staining my T-shirt. Like most Chinese kids, we were brought up to be ultimate eaters, and not much made us squeamish.

Roadside shacks with corrugated-iron roofs, dark and noisy within, served French toast piled high on melamine plates—bread dipped in egg and deep-fried, a pitcher of corn syrup to pour over it on the table. At lunchtimes, businessmen would fling their ties over their shoulders while ladies folded napkins onto their laps to come away pristine and ready to go back to work. Strong tea made with sweet evaporated milk and then poured at a height to make a frothy top was how I learned to love caffeine.

Strip-lit cafés served junky instant noodles in salty broth, perhaps topped with a slice of fried SPAM, or a fried egg nestling on top. I still love SPAM, as you might come to realize. The best chicken you could eat came from places like this, fried with a drizzle of soy sauce and a slick of ginger and scallion oil. It was for everyone— the poor, the wealthy. Everyone in Hong Kong had a passion for food. This wasn't just food you'd eat as a guilty pleasure; it was part of Hong Kong culture.

Sundays were spent in cavernous, brightly lit restaurants for the family dim sum brunch. Back then, my grandfather would arrive first, far earlier than everyone else, to nab the best table. He'd read the paper, sip tea, and snack on a few egg rolls while our family gathered in dribs and drabs, noisily greeting one another and settling into their seats. Carts full of steamers were wheeled past, their drivers calling out their contents. I would poke my head inquisitively in their direction and the ladies pushing them would cock a lid so that I could steal a glimpse inside. I'd gaze wide-eyed, nose wrinkled as elder aunties would choose a braised chicken's foot from the steamer for their bowl, only to suck all the skin off the bones and then delicately but deliberately spit all the bones out onto the tablecloth, chopsticks sometimes guiding the way. It was a real art, honed by many years of practice, and one I haven't yet mastered but perhaps something to look forward to in later life. The lazy Susan piled high with dishes constantly revolved and I soon learned not to spin it before my time; a sharp rap on the knuckles with a chopstick was all it took.

My grandmother lived with us for many of my formative years. She'd get us out of bed in the morning with a devastating wrench of the quilt cover, tell us off when my sister and I fought, and take us for secret snacks at McDonald's. If ever we expressed a particular fondness for an after-school snack, that was it; it would be ours every day until we pleaded for something new. Often we'd go to the wet markets with her. The people manning the stands were all familiar friends and they'd coo over my sister and ruffle my hair, teasing me for looking like a boy with my bowl haircut (thanks Mom). My grandmother would wander from stand to stand, selecting the fresh vegetables and picking up still-wriggling fish to inspect their freshness. A finger pointed at a particular chicken pacing nervously in a cage would mean the end for it; she always instructed me to look away when it was dealt with, and I disobeyed only once. The chicken soup that evening was difficult to swallow.

In the kitchen, though, we were often shooed away. Hong Kong kitchens are never spacious—there were always pots and pans bubbling away, a wok sizzling, a rice cooker steaming. We were relegated to the living room to be amused by the television. I learned no culinary skills from my grandmother, much to my dismay, but what was imparted to me was the joy of eating.

I moved to the UK when I was 13 and I soon realized that the food I grew up with was unobtainable in rural Suffolk. My poor mother was left to fend for herself in a foreign country with two children while my father tied up all the paperwork back in Hong Kong, and not being much of a cook herself and rather homesick too, we ate a lot of Chinese takeouts. We were aghast by the nuclear-orange sweet and sour chicken, and repulsed by the sickly-sweet crispy chili beef, but at least some of the noodle dishes and others that were served with rice were passable. I threw myself into British life. Those dishes now hold a special place in my heart.

By the time I left home at 18 and moved to London, I really did miss the meals of my childhood. Nostalgic flashbacks would come unbidden. On some winter days, I wouldn't be able to get the thought of tender, melting beef brisket slow-braised with star anise and cinnamon out of my head. Other times I actively craved that sunshine-yellow egg custard tart; I'd positively drool over the memory of still-warm flaky pastry, the just-set custard dissolving in my mouth. It was unbearable.

So I began researching recipes for those dishes I missed, from comforting home-style cooking to fancier restaurant dishes. This took me to the heart of Chinatown, and tentatively I studied labels on jars, bought odd-looking ingredients on a whim, and had to look up how on earth I'd use them once I got home. It was an experimental and lengthy process, but I fell in love with the Asian supermarkets. Not only did they provide me with access to delicious food, each trip was a journey down memory lane—I could pick up particular brands and squeal, "I remember this!"

I started my blog, Hollow Legs, in March 2008 so that I'd be able to document the recipes I was discovering. The name came from a nickname my parents gave me for my insatiable appetite (commonly known as greediness). I trawled forums, blogs, recipe sites, and the like to get an idea of the recipes I was after so that I could experiment with them all, borrowing ideas from some and embellishing others with my own touches—often, more chili was added to spicy dishes, more vinegar to sour. My taste buds seem to love those flavors the most. Slowly but surely I learned to cook. It was very much trial and error—a LOT of error, aided by some cursing—but the Internet is a wonderful thing. YouTube videos showed me various cooking techniques, while other blogs with step-by-step instructions or pictures helped me out with the rest. The Asians are an enthusiastic bunch, not only loving their food but having an incredible desire to share their recipes.

Over time, I grew more adventurous; I branched out into other cuisines, such as Korean, Japanese, and Thai. Though I admire Western cooking and I am seriously fiendish for pasta, it never quite took me as much as Asian food did, and still does. It fascinates me; bright, perky, in-your-face flavors dominate the Asian cuisines, and they take no prisoners. Several trips to Thailand, Malaysia, and Singapore cemented this fascination, while the Asian supermarkets, be they in Chinatown or online, enabled me to make the recipes I loved the most at home in the UK.

This book is a guide to the Asian supermarket and the treasures you can find within. The supermarkets themselves are often described as intimidating, daunting, or confusing. They're usually big spaces, packed with packages, jars, cans, and spices in varying degrees of comprehensibility. My hope is that in sharing the main attributes of common ingredients via the recipes here, the intimidation will lessen and you will gain confidence in Asian food, as I did.

This isn't supposed to be an educational tome, tangled in the authenticity of cuisines. There are some classic recipes remade to my take in here, but you'll also find that I've downright rejected authenticity in a couple of the recipes to make way for what tastes good—that's what it's all about, isn't it? It's what I hope to be a fun, accessible book that showcases ingredients used often in Asian cooking. Each chapter has a list and summary of things you might find in each aisle—a sort of index—so that after a quick glance for reference you can find what you're looking for more easily or which category something belongs in.

I can't say that after cooking from this book you will become an expert in Asian cuisine (is anyone, really?), but that isn't really my intention either. What I hope for is that you'll feel the excitement I get when I walk into an Asian supermarket; a sense of flavorsome possibility, and a feeling of adventure in experimenting with everything inside them.

BASIC EQUIPMENT

WOK & LID

The humble wok is probably the most important piece of equipment in the Asian kitchen. Don't bother with the expensive, fancy, nonstick coated types; all you need is a flat-bottomed stainless steel one that you can buy from most Asian supermarkets, some cooking oil, and a little time to make it nonstick.

Firstly, open all the doors and windows of your kitchen, since this can get a little smoky. Use a brush or a sponge with plenty of soapy water and give the wok a good scrub, to remove the machine-oil residue. Dry the wok and then place it on the stove on the highest heat. Move the wok around so that the heat reaches the sides all over—you will see it will start changing color. Add 3 to 4 tablespoons of vegetable oil to the wok and swirl it around carefully, using a piece of paper towel reach the more difficult places. Continue heating like this for another minute or two, then remove from the heat and wipe any residual oil out. Let cool for 10 minutes, then place back on the heat with another tablespoon of oil and repeat the process until you have a uniform brown/black patina developing.

Don't stir-fry any starches, such as rice or noodles, until you have used the wok a few more times and have really developed that patina further. After you have used your wok, clean it with water—no soap or detergent—and a soft brush, then place it back on the heat to dry, wipe around the inside of it with a little cooking oil, and let it cool. This prevents it from rusting. You soon get into the habit.

DOLSOT

A dolsot is a traditional Korean granite stone bowl, used for dishes such as bibimbap (rice topped with ingredients, followed by a raw egg that cooks in the residual heat of the bowl—most prized for the crispy rice that forms at the bottom of the bowl). When heated on the stove or in the oven, the granite retains the heat well, and so cooks the dish more effectively. The dolsot should be heated gradually to avoid cracking the bowl.

CHINESE CLAY POTS

These usually come in various sizes with a lid. They should be soaked overnight in a sink full of water before their first use, and like the dolsot, should be heated gradually after being soaked in cold water for 15 minutes first. The Chinese believe that cooking in clay pots give the dish a distinct flavor and keeps the nutrients within. Clay pots are mainly used for one-pot dishes, such as Bo Kho or Braised Chicken, Broccoli, & Shiitake Mushrooms (*see page 206*).

RICE COOKER

You don't have to have one of these, but it's worth it if you are going to be cooking a lot of Asian food. It frees up stove space, you don't have to worry about anything boiling over, and it keeps rice warm for as long as you like.

STEAMER

Either a metal steamer insert for a saucepan or a bamboo steamer are ideal. A metal steamer insert for the wok is also great for steaming larger ingredients.

CLEAVER

A simple chopping cleaver from the Asian supermarket is great for when you need to chop through meat or poultry bones or carcasses. Otherwise, a chef's knife has served me well.

COOKING CHOPSTICKS

These are particularly good for moving delicate ingredients around, far more so than tongs.

METAL SPATULA

As well as cooking chopsticks, a metal spatula is handy for moving food around at high heat.

CUTTING BOARD

Buying a large, sturdy wooden cutting board is a good idea; Asian cooking often involves a lot of chopping of different items, and for efficiency I like to have all my ingredients for cooking lined up and ready to go.

MORTAR & PESTLE

A sturdy mortar and pestle is very handy for preparing Asian food. They are useful to make garlic or ginger pastes, or dressings. Look for a high-sided granite one; they're best for keeping ingredients in one place, so you can go to town with the pestling. You can use a mini chopper, but many say a curry paste made by hand is far superior.

BASIC INGREDIENTS

Loading up with supplies for an Asian kitchen cupboard can be a bit daunting, but once you have these items on hand, it means that for each individual recipe you will only need to pick up fresh ingredients and a flavoring or two.

LIGHT SOY SAUCE

This is the most commonly used seasoning in Japanese and Chinese cuisine, its primary function being to add salt to dishes. It's worth buying the best quality you can, since it's used so often and there is a real difference in quality. I favor Pearl River Bridge Premium Deluxe. Tamari is a gluten-free alternative for celiacs.

DARK SOY SAUCE

This soy sauce is used sparingly, often for a hint of color and a caramel-like depth of flavor, so you can start off with a smaller bottle.

OYSTER SAUCE

Thick, glossy, and slightly sweet, oyster sauce is frequently used to give sauces body, or to season vegetables. When choosing which brand to buy, look for the highest percentage of oyster extract in the ingredients.

FISH SAUCE

Mostly used in Thai, Cambodian, Laotian, Filipino, and Vietnamese food, fish sauce is an amber-colored liquid that is fermented with salt. It is often used to cook with, but is also used in dressings and dipping sauces. The quality of different fish sauce brands varies; I prefer Three Crabs for a more subtle and smooth flavor.

CHINKIANG BLACK VINEGAR

Used mostly in Southern Chinese dishes, Chinkiang black vinegar has a smoky flavor with a hint of sweetness. To preserve its delicacy, it's usually added to a dish at the end of cooking, and is also used for dipping sauces and marinades.

RICE VINEGAR

Clear and white, rice vinegar is much stronger and more acidic than black vinegar, though still more mellow than Western counterparts.

RICE WINES

Shaoxing rice wine is used the most in this book, but it's also worth picking up some cooking sake if you come across it, for Japanese dishes.

SESAME OIL

Toasted sesame oil is frequently used to flavor a dish, rather than to cook things in. The anomaly is when it comes to Korean food, where sesame oil is often used to cook with but usually untoasted for a milder flavor. If you don't want to buy both, go for toasted and mix it with a little vegetable oil when preparing Korean dishes.

CHILI OIL

Make your own by heating dried chili flakes in vegetable or peanut oil. You can also grind together dried chiles, salt, and garlic with a mortar and pestle, then slowly cook the mixture in vegetable oil until red-hued and infused. Alternatively, there are lots of great ready-made chili oils you can buy. I like jars with sediment in them, for extra kick, and I always check the label for ones without MSG (monosodium glutamate—*see page 16*) or E numbers.

FRAGRANT JASMINE RICE

You can use basmati, you can use brown, but white fragrant jasmine rice is the most commonly used rice in Asian cooking. If you're serious about Asian food, I'd urge you to get a rice cooker (*see page 11*). But otherwise, follow the cooking method on page 47.

GINGER, GARLIC & SCALLIONS

I am never without these three ingredients, often considered to be the holy trinity of Chinese cooking, and garlic is used liberally throughout Asia. So it's worth keeping these items on hand at all times.

WHITE PEPPER

You can buy whole white peppercorns, but the ground stuff is pungent too and much easier to handle.

COOKING OIL

A lot of my recipes start off with "Heat the oil in a wok." My oil of choice is vegetable or sunflower oil; olive oil, though healthier, is too flavorsome for Asian cooking, and peanut oil, which many traditional cooks use, goes rancid comparatively quickly.

CORNSTARCH & POTATO STARCH

These are used a lot in marinades and to thicken sauces. While most of the time the two are interchangeable, potato starch yields crisper deep-fried food.

DRIED SHIITAKE MUSHROOMS

These are often added to dishes or used as a flavoring. Always buy them whole and look for those with a white fissured flower pattern on the cap; these are more expensive, but better quality. To use, soak in water overnight for the best flavor, but if you're in a rush, you can soak them in boiling water for 30 minutes without too much detriment. Always discard the stem before using, and you can strain the mushroom water to use as a stock.

CHAPTER

SAUCES & CONDIMENTS

SAUCES & CONDIMENTS

Many Asian sauces and condiments head for one objective; Japanese miso paste, Sichuan chili bean paste, and Korean doenjang and gochujang are all made by fermenting soybeans in order to build a base layer of that fifth taste that accompanies the other four of sweet, salty, bitter, and sour—umami. The best way to describe it is deeply savory; yes, it's salty, but it's more than that. It's what makes your dish go from tasting good to tasting excellent. MSG (monosodium glutamate), which is now a dirty word, is chemically manufactured umami, but this chemical compound occurs naturally in foods like tomatoes, mushrooms, and Parmesan cheese. Anchovies also have a high level of umami, which goes a little way to explaining the liberal uses of fish sauce, shrimp sauce, and shrimp paste in many cuisines. It is, in the simplest sense, deliciousness.

In an ideal world, we would be able to make everything we eat completely from scratch, without E numbers or preservatives, but in Asian cooking life is just too short to ferment your own soybeans and make your own soy sauce. All the following sauces and condiments are available in Asian supermarkets. Some brands are of higher quality than others, and when I'm shopping for them I tend to check the labels, since some have more E numbers than others.

I'm sure there are many soybean-based condiments, but the following are the ones that I've found to be most commonly available in my Asian supermarket snoopings, and those I use the most.

GOCHUJANG

This is Korean chili paste, made by fermenting soybeans with chile, salt, and glutinous (sticky) rice in the sun. Often sold in a red plastic tub, the paste is smooth, vividly red, and tacky. As far as chili heat goes, it's fairly mild and quite sweet. It's used to flavor soups and stews, added to dressings, and also makes a mean coating for crisp-fried chicken, affectionately coined KFC (Korean fried chicken).

DOENJANG

Literally meaning "thick paste" in Korean, rich brown doenjang is fermented soybeans without the chile and is often sold in a coarser-textured form than gochujang, though it's just as sticky. It has a slightly yeasty, nutty aroma to it and a deep savory edge, and is normally mixed with other pastes to make a dip, or dissolved in stews.

CHILI BEAN PASTE

Called doubanjiang, this paste is the basis of many Sichuanese dishes, and is very spicy. It has a looser, rougher texture than its Korean counterpart, and does not have the latter's sweetness. It is sometimes made with fava beans as well as soybeans.

YELLOW BEAN PASTE

Contrary to its name, this is a smooth, dark brown sauce. Salty and slightly sweet in flavor, it is used most commonly in noodle and stir-fried dishes in Chinese cooking.

FERMENTED BLACK BEANS

You can buy salted, fermented black beans whole, usually with ginger, or already ground up and mashed into a sauce. I prefer the whole beans. They last forever in the cupboard and are more versatile because some dishes don't require them to be pulverized into a paste. Again, these are made by fermenting and salting black soybeans. They're incredibly salty, so it's best to give them a rinse before you use them to get rid of the excess salt and to plump them up a little. Black beans are used as a flavoring, and you can add them to stir-fried vegetables and meat, mash them with some water to make a sauce, or scatter a few over fish before you steam it.

HOI SIN SAUCE

Known as the barbecue sauce of the Chinese world, hoi sin is sweet and ubiquitous, and slightly trashy, thanks to its misattribution as plum sauce for roast duck and pancakes (though I find it works perfectly well used that way). It's dark to almost black, sticky, thick, and, you've guessed it, made with soybeans. It also contains sesame, garlic, salt, vinegar, and sometimes chiles, to flavor it.

MISO

The backbone of Japanese cuisine, miso comes in many guises; some varieties are made with fermented rice, others with fermented barley, but most types commercially available in the West are made from soybeans. Miso comes in various grades, from white (shiro), the mildest and sweetest miso, to red (aka), which is saltier and more intense, as well as in various forms depending on the Japanese region of origin. You are unlikely to have much choice other than color, unless you are in a serious Japanese supermarket. So, the rule of thumb is that red is much stronger and saltier than white, therefore use it sparingly. Miso can be used to make dressings, soups, and sauces; try not to bring it to a boil, because all the health benefits are ruined by excessive heat.

SHRIMP PASTES

There are many different variants of shrimp paste, ranging from solid blocks and pastes with textures like molasses to very liquid and runny kinds. Confusingly, they are almost all called shrimp paste.

BELACAN

Otherwise known as shrimp paste, belacan is sold as a dark brown, solid block. It's made with fermented ground shrimp and salt, and is most commonly used in Thai, Malaysian, Laotian, Cambodian, Vietnamese, and Filipino cuisines. Essential in many curries and sauces, it's usually cooked before consumption. It smells horrible when you give it a sniff out of the package (a recurring theme, you may find), but once it's cooked it transforms into a mouthwatering flavor—umami in action.

HAE KO

Also called petis udang, this shrimp paste is thick and gloopy like molasses. It's made with sugar for a sweeter consistency, and is mainly served as a condiment in Malaysian cooking with dishes such as popiah rolls and assam laksa.

FINE SHRIMP SAUCE

Also called mam tom in Vietnamese, this sauce is smooth with a grayish-purple color. It is a very liquid paste and is probably the smelliest of them all. It's mixed with chili, garlic, and lime to make a Vietnamese dipping sauce for seafood, and also for marinating meat.

FISH SAUCE

Fish sauce is integral to a number of Asian cuisines, such as Thai, Cambodian, and Vietnamese. Made by fermenting fish with salt, it is used as a seasoning in cooking and in dressings, and as a dipping sauce. It, too, contains that essential fifth flavor of umami. Some can be harsher and more pungent than others. So, when using fish sauce, use the quantities given as a guide only and taste as you go along.

SESAME PASTE

This is not made with soybeans or fish! Sesame paste comes in two forms: light, which you may be more familiar with as tahini; and a dark, rich brown version, which is roasted sesame paste. Both have their uses, but I prefer the latter for a more complex flavor. Sesame paste is mostly used in salad dressings, or for tossing with noodles.

The glorious thing about many Korean stews is that the method generally consists of "chop, dump in pot, and cook." Perfect for lazy cooks, like me on a weeknight. Or a weekend. Given the short cooking time for this, it has a surprisingly deep flavor. Be sure to use chicken thighs, since the darker meat is far more flavorsome than the breast meat.

DAK DORITANG

Bring a saucepan of water to a boil and drop the chicken pieces in. Simmer for 2 minutes. Drain and rinse the pan and the chicken thoroughly.

Meanwhile, combine all the sauce ingredients in a bowl, add the chicken, and toss well.

Place the chicken and sauce back in the clean pan and bring to a simmer. Stir in the potatoes and onions, cover, and simmer for 10 minutes. Add the carrots and toss in the sauce well, cover again, and let simmer for another 20 minutes. If it's looking a little dry, add more water, but this is supposed to be nice and thick.

Remove the lid, stir, and add the beans or greenery, then simmer gently for another 15 minutes. Serve over steamed white rice with the sliced scallions garnishing each serving.

4 large bone-in chicken thighs (get your butcher to chop each into 2 for you, or get your cleaver out)

6 new potatoes, sliced in half so that they are bite-size

2 white onions, each chopped into 6

2 carrots, peeled and coarsely chopped

handful of green snap beans, or any greenery you have, really

4 scallions, diagonally sliced, to garnish

For the sauce:

2 tablespoons gochujang (see page 16)

3 tablespoons coarse Korean chili powder (this is not blow-your-head-off stuff but gives it the red color so, if you use a different chili powder be careful with quantities)

5 garlic cloves, minced

2-inch piece of fresh ginger root, peeled and minced

3 tablespoons light soy sauce

1 tablespoon superfine sugar

1 tablespoon Shaoxing rice wine

2 tablespoons tomato ketchup (yes, really)

¼ cup water

This jjigae (Korean for "stew") is a staple in Korean home cooking, and is very customizable. You can replace the squid with shrimp or beef, and the broccoli with zucchini or squash. Great for a vegetable drawer clear-out.

DOENJANG JJIGAE

SERVES 4

1 cup fragrant jasmine rice

1 cup water

3-inch square sheet of dried kombu (*see page 188*)

1 teaspoon sesame oil

4 garlic cloves, minced

1 small onion, diced

¼ cup doenjang (*see page 16*)

1 potato, peeled and quartered

3½ oz daikon (Asian radish), peeled and cut into bite-size chunks

half a block (5½ to 6 oz) soft silken tofu (bean curd), drained, patted dry with paper towels, and cut into cubes

3 stems of green sprouting broccoli

1 large squid tube or **2** small, cut into bite-size diamond shapes, skin scored

1 scallion, thinly sliced diagonally, to garnish

Put the rice in a saucepan, add the water, and rub the rice grains between your hands until the water turns milky. Drain the rice water into another saucepan and bring to a simmer with the kombu. Simmer gently for 15 minutes. Add more water to the rice and put the rice on to cook, either in a rice cooker or a saucepan (*see page 11 and 47*).

Heat the sesame oil in a saucepan or dolsot (a traditional Korean stone bowl used for cooking stews and rice dishes—*see page 11*). Add the garlic and onion and fry for 5 minutes, or until the onion has softened. Remove the kombu from the rice water and add the liquid. Add the doenjang, whisking as you go to remove any lumps. Add the potato and the daikon, cover, and simmer gently on low heat for 30 minutes.

Add the tofu and simmer for another 10 minutes, stirring gently. Place the broccoli in a layer on top of the broth along with the squid, cover, and simmer gently for another 5 minutes. By this point the broccoli will be tender and the squid will have curled. Serve with the cooked rice, garnished with the scallion.

You can buy ready-made ssamjang sauce (it most commonly comes in a green container), but since you have already gone to the trouble of buying both gochujang and doenjang, there seems little need for another space invader for the fridge. Use this sauce for crudités, and bo ssam—a famous Korean meal of barbecued meats placed in a lettuce leaf with some rice or kimchi. You can also thin this down with a light-flavored oil to dress strong leaves, like arugula, mizuna, or watercress.

SSAMJANG SAUCE

SERVES 4

Mix all the ingredients together in a bowl until well combined.

¼ cup doenjang (*see page 16*)
1½ tablespoons gochujang (*see page 16*)
1 scallion, minced
1 garlic clove, minced
3 shallots, minced
2 teaspoons liquid honey
2 teaspoons sesame oil
2 teaspoons white sesame seeds, toasted

This dish, of course, has nothing to do with Bolognese as you or I know it. There is no spaghetti or red wine anywhere near this, and no tomatoes. In fact, the only similarities are that it is made by simmering meat in a sauce and then dressing noodles with it. But I'm still going with the name Chinese Spag Bol. The yellow bean sauce is the base of the dish, and the longer the meat simmers in it, the more flavorsome it becomes. The addition of fresh, crunchy vegetables stirred in at the end makes it feel deceptively light. You've been warned.

 SERVES 4

CHINESE SPAG BOL

2 tablespoons cooking oil, divided

2 free-range eggs, beaten

2 scallions, white parts minced, green parts sliced into rings

5 garlic cloves, minced

2 teaspoons peeled and minced fresh ginger root

14 oz fatty ground pork

3 tablespoons yellow bean paste (see page 16)

1 teaspoon light soy sauce

1 teaspoon dark soy sauce

1 tablespoon hoi sin sauce

½ cup water

2 tablespoons Shaoxing rice wine

1 carrot, peeled

½ cucumber

10½ oz fresh Shanghai noodles

Heat 1 tablespoon of the cooking oil in a wok or nonstick skillet over medium heat until shimmering. Add the beaten eggs and cook until set to make a thin omelet. Transfer to a plate and set aside.

Heat the rest of the oil in the wok over medium heat, add the scallion whites, garlic, and ginger and stir-fry until fragrant. Then add the ground pork, breaking up any clumps with your fingers, and cook until browned. Add the yellow bean paste, soy sauces, and hoi sin sauce along with the water and Shaoxing rice wine and simmer for 30 minutes, stirring occasionally. If it's looking a little dry, add a touch more water.

Meanwhile, julienne the carrot and cucumber and set aside. Roll the omelet up and slice finely.

Cook the noodles in a large saucepan of boiling water for a minute, then drain and place in a big serving bowl. Pour the meat sauce on top, then add the vegetables and omelet and stir to combine. Garnish with the rings of green scallion and serve.

I'm sure that as you read this recipe you'll think 'Boy, what a lot of fuss', and perhaps it is, but it's also incredibly delicious. It combines the best flavors you can get with chili bean paste—spicy, sour, a little sweet. A whole fish is a real centerpiece, but you can also use fillets, although you lose the most delicious morsel that you, as Chief Cook, get dibs on—that nugget of cheek, just below the eye.

DEEP-FRIED WHOLE FISH IN CHILI BEAN SAUCE

SERVES 2 TO 4 WITH OTHER DISHES

1 whole sea bream, rainbow trout, or red snapper, weighing about 1¾ lb, gutted and scaled

1 tablespoon Shaoxing rice wine

4 garlic cloves

2-inch piece of fresh ginger root, peeled

1 scallion

3½ cups cooking oil

cornstarch, for dusting

2 to 3 tablespoons chili bean paste (*see page 16*), depending on how salty your chili bean paste is (I usually go for 3)

2 teaspoons superfine sugar

⅔ cup water

2 teaspoons Chinkiang black vinegar

1 teaspoon potato starch, mixed with **1 tablespoon** cold water

Cut 3 slits into the flesh of the fish at a right angle to the spine, on both sides. Splash with the rice wine, turn the fish over, and let it sit while you work on the sauce ingredients.

Mince the garlic and ginger very finely together. Slice the scallion into rings and set aside for the garnish.

Heat the oil in a wok until a bread crumb dropped into it sizzles immediately. Pat the fish dry and coat with cornstarch, dusting off the excess. Fry on one side for 5 minutes, then use a lifter and a metal spatula to carefully turn it over. The cornstarch should have prevented the skin from sticking. Fry for another 4 minutes. You may need to tilt the wok, or spoon the oil over the head and tail, if the fish is particularly long. Remove carefully and place on a plate lined with paper towels.

Drain the oil into a heatproof container, wipe any cornstarch residue out of the wok, then pour 2 tablespoons of the oil back into the wok. Add the chili bean paste and fry over medium heat until it is fragrant, then add the garlic and ginger and stir-fry for 2 minutes. Add the sugar and the water, and stir to combine. Carefully put the fish into the wok and braise gently for 5 minutes, spooning the sauce over the fish where it doesn't reach.

By now your fish should be cooked, unless it's really large, in which case put the lid on for a few more minutes until it has cooked—test by poking with a chopstick near the spine; if it's cooked, the flesh will come away easily. Transfer the fish to a serving platter. Add the vinegar to the sauce (this is done last to preserve the flavor). Stir the potato-starch solution into the wok and simmer until it has thickened, then remove from the heat. Spoon the sauce over and around the fish, and garnish with the scallion rings.

This is probably one of the most classic and ubiquitous Cantonese dishes, and when done well, black bean sauce is salty and earthy with a funk of the beans' fermented-ness about it. You can use a whole bell pepper of the one color, but I like the slight bitterness of the green bell pepper. You can also substitute chicken or pork for the beef. The baking-soda marinade is a little restaurant trick, used to tenderize the meat.

SERVES **4** WITH OTHER DISHES

BEEF IN BLACK BEAN SAUCE

10½ oz beef rump

2 tablespoons oyster sauce

1 tablespoon cornstarch

½ teaspoon baking soda

¼ cup cooking oil

3 garlic cloves, minced

1-inch piece of fresh ginger root, peeled and minced

3 tablespoons fermented black beans (see page 16), rinsed well and then drained, chopped, and mashed with the back of a spoon

1 large red chile, sliced into rings

½ red bell pepper, cored, seeded, and chopped into bite-size pieces

½ green bell pepper, cored, seeded, and chopped into bite-size pieces

2 tablespoons Shaoxing rice wine

1 teaspoon dark soy sauce

1 teaspoon superfine sugar

2 scallions, white parts sliced in half lengthwise, green parts sliced into rings

3 tablespoons stock or water

Slice the beef into thin strips against the grain. Mix the oyster sauce, cornstarch, and baking soda together in a bowl. Add the beef strips, toss to coat, and then cover the bowl with plastic wrap. Let marinate for at least 20 minutes while you prepare the rest of the ingredients.

Add the cooking oil to a wok and heat over high heat until just below smoking. Add the beef and stir-fry briskly, separating the strips out, for 1 minute, or until browned. It will sizzle a lot, so be careful. Transfer to a plate and set aside.

Drain all but 1 tablespoon of the oil from the wok. Add the garlic and ginger and stir-fry until fragrant. Add the black beans and chile and carry on stir-frying. Add the bell peppers, rice wine, soy sauce, sugar, the whites of the scallions, and the stock or water. Cook, stirring, for about 5 minutes, or until the peppers are almost tender.

Return the beef to the wok and stir-fry for a minute more. At this point the sauce should be thickening a little and becoming glossy. Take off the heat and garnish with the green scallion rings.

This Japanese salad is traditionally made with just sesame seeds, but I've upped the flavor factor with three helpings of sesame. The rich, dark brown sesame paste gives it a helping hand to make it creamy and filling, and not at all like the cold vegetable side that it is. Serve it alongside Chicken Katsu Curry (*see page 194*) or other hearty meat dishes.

JAPANESE SPINACH and CUCUMBER SALAD

SERVES 2 AS A SIDE DISH

If using fresh spinach, bring a saucepan of water to a boil. Have a large bowl of cold water with ice cubes ready nearby. Chop the stems off the spinach and add them to the boiling water, followed by the leaves 10 seconds later. Remove from the heat immediately, drain, and plunge the leaves and stems into the iced water.

Meanwhile, slice the cucumber into thick matchstick shapes. Put the dark sesame paste, soy sauce, rice vinegar, and sesame oil into a clean jar, screw on the lid, and shake to mix, or mix together in a bowl. You may need a tablespoon of water to loosen it—it should be the texture of a thick salad dressing, like a Caesar.

Drain the blanched spinach and squeeze dry in a dish towel; likewise if using frozen. Using your fingers, combine with the cucumber, then combine with the dressing, mixing well so that it is all coated.

Pile onto a serving dish and garnish with the toasted sesame seeds.

10½ oz fresh spinach leaves, rinsed well, or frozen whole leaf spinach, defrosted in hot water, drained, and squeezed dry

1 cucumber, peeled and seeded

2 tablespoons dark sesame paste (*see page 17*)

1 tablespoon light soy sauce

1 teaspoon rice vinegar

1 tablespoon sesame oil

1 tablespoon white sesame seeds, toasted

Let's get one thing straight. Shrimp sauce absolutely stinks. It smells like a thousand rotten shrimp, crammed into a jar. It is (probably) that. If you open the jar and take a sniff, your head will jerk back, brow furrowed, as if you've been slapped. Something strange happens when you cook with it, though; it changes aroma, and becomes mouthwatering. It smells of the seaside, with added toastiness. It becomes appetizing. If there's any way to get you on board with this death-paste, it's fried chicken. I don't know anyone who doesn't like fried chicken. Juicy meat and a crunchy, flavorsome exterior are key criteria for success.

CHINESE FRIED CHICKEN

SERVES 8 AS A SNACK

2¼ lb mixture of chicken thighs and wings

3 tablespoons fine shrimp sauce (*see page 17*)

2 teaspoons superfine sugar

2 garlic cloves, mashed

2 teaspoons ginger juice (grate fresh ginger root and squeeze the pulp to release the juice)

2 tablespoons Shaoxing rice wine

2 tablespoons oyster sauce

½ cup potato starch

3 cups cooking oil

Chop the chicken thighs in half through the bone with a cleaver and place in a large bowl. Take each chicken wing and separate the upper wing from the lower wing and wing tip. Add to the bowl.

Mix together the shrimp sauce, sugar, garlic, ginger juice, Shaoxing wine, and oyster sauce, then use it to coat the chicken, mixing well. Cover and let marinate in the fridge for at least 6 hours, or overnight.

Ten minutes before cooking, add the potato starch to the chicken and stir well to combine.

Heat the oil in a wok or saucepan to 350°F. Fry the chicken pieces, in batches, for 8 to 10 minutes, or until crisp and browned, turning once. Transfer to a wire rack to drain.

Serve with **CHILI & GINGER SAUCE** (*see page 64*) for dipping, or sriracha (*see page 109 for homemade, or use ready-made*).

We've already ascertained the incredible stench of shrimp sauce. So, with that in mind, I will ask you to open all your windows, turn the extraction fan on, and apologize to anyone in the vicinity, because stench is no reason to turn down something delicious. In this recipe, the tender squid turns a grayish hue, and the celery is essential in bringing a little vibrancy to the dish.

STIR-FRIED SQUID *with* CELERY IN SHRIMP SAUCE

SERVES

2

WITH OTHER DISHES

6 oz squid, cleaned
2 celery stalks
1-inch piece of fresh ginger root
3 garlic cloves
1 red chile
1 scallion
2 tablespoons cooking oil
2 tablespoons water
1 tablespoon Shaoxing rice wine
1 teaspoon fine shrimp sauce
(*see page 17*)
1 teaspoon sugar

Cut the squid into largish pieces because they will curl up as they cook. Using a sharp knife, score the flesh on one side in a crisscross pattern, but not so deep as to cut all the way through.

Trim the celery, give it a good wash, and then use a vegetable peeler to peel off the outer stringy bits. Slice in half and cut each half lengthwise into quarters, then slice into 1½-inch batons.

Peel the skin off the ginger and mince it with the garlic. Chop the chili coarsely, removing the seeds if you prefer a milder dish. Slice the scallion diagonally.

Add the oil to a wok over high heat and heat until just below smoking. Add the ginger, garlic, chile, and celery and stir-fry briskly for 1 minute. Add the water, and then stir-fry until it evaporates. Then add the squid, rice wine, shrimp sauce, and sugar all at once. Stir-fry the mixture, moving everything constantly around the pan for 3 to 4 minutes, or until the squid is cooked. Remove from the heat and toss the scallion through. Serve immediately.

For a dish with so few ingredients, this is insanely delicious. It might be partly something to do with the fatty richness of pork belly, or the basic human love of sugar or the savory hit of fish sauce, but combined it is a beautiful thing. I particularly love the gelatinous quality of the skin when it is slowly braised, though some get squeamish about it. Roll your eyes at them until they at least try a little, and then rejoice when they see the light.

CARAMEL PORK BELLY

Add the oil to a small skillet on medium heat and brown the pork cubes on all sides. It doesn't need to be cooked through at this stage. Remove from the skillet and drain on paper towels.

In a saucepan just big enough to hold the pork, heat the sugar over low heat until it has dissolved and caramelized to a deep golden color, swirling the pan once it has started to melt but resisting the temptation to stir.

Remove from the heat and stir in 3 tablespoons warm water, being careful to stay clear of the spattering, burning-hot caramel. If the sugar should seize into a hard state, bring to a boil to return the caramel to a liquid form.

Stir the pork into the caramel, then stir in the fish sauce with another 3 tablespoons of water. Cover and cook very gently for about an hour until the meat is tender, turning the pork cubes halfway through the cooking time. Add the ground pepper, put the lid back on, and cook for another 5 minutes.

Serve with plain rice and steamed vegetables (*see page 84*), or the **SMACKED CUCUMBER SALAD** below.

1 teaspoon cooking oil

1 lb pork belly slices with skin, cut into bite-size cubes

3 tablespoons superfine sugar

2½ tablespoons fish sauce

½ teaspoon ground black pepper

---

1 large cucumber

2 teaspoons salt

2½ tablespoons rice vinegar

3 garlic cloves, minced

2 teaspoons jaggery (palm sugar)

2 teaspoons chili oil

2 teaspoons toasted sesame oil

1 teaspoon light soy sauce

SMACKED CUCUMBER SALAD

Lay the cucumber on a cutting board and smack lightly with a cleaver or a rolling pin. Chop coarsely and add to a colander, sprinkling with the salt. Let stand for 30 minutes, and then rinse and pat dry with paper towels.

Mix together the vinegar, garlic, sugar, chili oil, sesame oil, and soy sauce in a bowl. Add the cucumber to the mixture and let stand to soak up the flavors for 10 minutes before serving.

Nuoc cham is a Vietnamese dipping sauce, commonly served with noodle salads, egg rolls, summer rolls, and banh xeo (a crêpe-like pancake stuffed with bean sprouts and protein). Essentially, this sauce should be made with the component parts as you prefer. So keep tasting and adding them according to your taste, because you might like it more sour, more sweet, or more or less spicy. This is how I like mine.

GRILLED EGGPLANTS *with* NUOC CHAM

SERVES 2 WITH OTHER DISHES

3 Asian eggplants, or use **1** large eggplant, cut into fingers

¼ cup vegetable oil

½ handful of mint

handful of fresh cilantro

1 quantity Nuoc Cham (*see below*)

handful of toasted cashews, coarsely crushed

Slice the Asian eggplants (if using) lengthwise into quarters, keeping the stem intact so that it holds the eggplant together. Heat the oil in a wok until almost smoking, then turn the heat down to medium and fry the eggplants well, turning occasionally. Do not burn. Transfer the eggplants to a baking dish. Cook under a preheated medium broiler for 20 minutes, turning the eggplants halfway through.

Chop the mint finely, and the cilantro leaves coarsely. Set aside. (If you have roots on your cilantro stalks, wash them well, chop them finely, and add them to the mortar to be ground into the nuoc cham sauce.)

To assemble, place the eggplants in a serving dish while warm, top with the mint and cilantro, and dress with the nuoc cham. Finally, scatter the dish with the cashews to serve.

NUOC CHAM

SERVES 2

1 fat garlic clove

2 teaspoons soft dark brown sugar

1 red bird's-eye chile (use more if you like it really hot, less if you don't)

juice of 1 lime

2 tablespoons fish sauce, or to taste

2 tablespoons water, or to taste

Peel the garlic clove and crush with the sugar using a mortar and pestle until it is a smooth paste. Seed the chile, chop it coarsely, and then add it to the mortar and give it a good pounding. Add the lime juice and mix well. Add 1 tablespoon of the fish sauce and taste. Add 1 tablespoon water and taste. Keep doing this until you have the desired piquancy or pungency. Remember that you can always add but you can't take away.

Hoi sin sauce has that heady, fruity sweetness that goes perfectly with pork, and becomes beautifully sticky when roasted or grilled. This is a ridiculously simple recipe with maximum flavor results; all you have to do is make sure your ribs are nice and fatty.

HOI SIN & GINGER PORK RIBS

SERVES 4

Put the ribs into a large dish. Blend all the sauce ingredients in a blender until you have a smooth consistency. Smear the sauce all over the ribs, using your fingers to make sure the ribs are completely covered. Cover the dish with plastic wrap and let marinate in the fridge overnight.

Preheat the oven to 400°F. Line a roasting pan with foil and set a rack onto it. Pour boiling water into the pan, lift the ribs out of the marinade, reserving what's left, and place the ribs on the rack, bone-side down. Roast for 30 minutes, then turn the oven down to 325°F, add more water if it's looking a little dry, and roast for another hour.

Simmer the remaining marinade in a small saucepan for 3 minutes. Chop the ribs into portions along the length of the bones and drizzle the sauce on top.

Serve with **CLOUD EAR FUNGUS & TOFU BAMBOO SALAD** (*see page 207*).

3 lb 5 oz rack of pork ribs

For the sauce:
1 onion, coarsely chopped
8 garlic cloves, peeled
6-inch piece of fresh ginger root, peeled
2/3 cup hoi sin sauce
1/4 cup orange juice
2 tablespoons sesame oil
2 tablespoons Shaoxing rice wine
2 tablespoons light soy sauce
1 tablespoon dark soy sauce
1 tablespoon tomato paste
1 teaspoon sherry vinegar
1 teaspoon black peppercorns

In Malaysian, Singaporean, and Indonesian cooking, "sambal" refers to a sauce, paste, or dip that includes chiles, be they cooked or fresh. There are many different kinds of sambal, and the recipe opposite is categorized by the addition of shrimp paste that is "tumis," which means stir-fried (the chiles and shrimp paste are cooked together with oil to make a rich and fragrant sauce). In fact, you can experiment with other ingredients using a base of chiles; combine them with tamarind paste to make a tart sambal assam, or add tomatoes for a milder, sweeter sambal. Try it with fried dried anchovies, or add raw chiles, tomatoes, and lime juice— almost like a Mexican salsa. Sambal oelek is the raw chili-paste version. This is a great dish for guests. The mackerel is stuffed to the brim with sambal and is perfect for people to pick at. Although traditionally it is deep-fried, I prefer to oil the skin and broil it, since it's far easier and you still get to enjoy crisp fish skin. Serve with bright stir-fried greens, some noodles, and steamed rice.

STUFFED SAMBAL MACKEREL

Preheat your broiler on the highest setting. Line up your mackerel with the head facing you and cut 2 slits down either side of the backbone of the fish. Use a teaspoon to stuff the slits with the Sambal Belacan. Smear any you have any left over into the cavity, too.

Line a roasting pan with foil and set a rack onto it. Oil both sides of the mackerel with your hands and place the fish on the rack so that it is standing up—you may have to prop it up with some foil rolled into a ball. Broil for 5 minutes with the mackerel at least 7 inches away from the heating element. Keep an eye on it—you don't want it to burn.

Carefully remove the foil props so that the mackerel lies on its side and broil for another 5 minutes, then turn it over and do the same again. By now the mackerel should be cooked and the flesh in the middle should pull away easily, but for mackerel on the large side, increase the cooking time to 8 to 10 minutes each side, turning the heat down a little so it doesn't burn.

Place the fish on a serving dish, squeeze the lime over it, and drizzle with the soy sauce to serve.

SERVES
2 TO 4
WITH OTHER DISHES

1 large or **2 small** whole mackerel, gutted

1 quantity Sambal Belacan (*see opposite*)

1 tablespoon cooking oil, for oiling

1 lime, halved, for squeezing

1 tablespoon light soy sauce

SAMBAL BELACAN

Snip the soaked chiles in half and discard the seeds. Pound them together in a mortar and pestle, along with the fresh red chiles, shallots, garlic, and lemon grass, adding 1 tablespoon of the cooking oil to help it along. The mixture should be quite fine so, if you happen to have a small blender, it will be much easier to use that for this step.

Toast the shrimp paste in a dry wok or skillet—it will be, shall we say, "aromatic"—then add to the chile mixture and blend or pound again until it is incorporated.

Add the remaining 2 tablespoons of oil to a wok on medium heat and add the mixture. Cook it for about 8 minutes, stirring often, until it has darkened (but not burned!) to a rich brown color. Stir in the jaggery and tamarind paste, simmer for another minute, and then remove from the heat. Scoop into a bowl to cool.

You can transfer this to a sterilized jar and cover with vegetable oil, then store in the fridge for up to a week.

MAKES

1 SMALL JAR

5 long, thin, dried red chiles, soaked in just-boiled water for 20 minutes, then drained

2 large, fresh red chiles, seeded and coarsely chopped

5 shallots, thinly sliced

3 garlic cloves, minced

1 lemon grass stalk, woody outer layers removed

3 tablespoons cooking oil, divided

½ tablespoon belacan (shrimp paste) (*see page 17*)

1 tablespoon jaggery (palm sugar)

½ tablespoon tamarind paste

I've mentioned before that belacan (shrimp paste) becomes much more palatable and less smelly once you cook it, and this dish proves it so, even with the gentlest of cooking. The pure, unflavored rice takes on the flavor of the shrimp paste, and if you're someone who likes a little variation in your meal, you'll probably enjoy customizing each mouthful using the different colorful bits and pieces lining your plate.

SERVES 2

THAI SHRIMP-PASTE RICE

6 oz boneless pork shoulder, sliced into thin strips

3 tablespoons jaggery (palm sugar)

3 tablespoons water

1½ tablespoons light soy sauce

2 teaspoons dark soy sauce

1 cup fragrant jasmine rice

3 tablespoons cooking oil, divided

2 free-range eggs, beaten with a dash of fish sauce

2 tablespoons dried shrimps, washed

1 Granny Smith apple or green mango

1 tablespoon belacan (shrimp paste) (see page 17), mashed with 1 tablespoon water

3½ oz green snap beans, blanched and diced

7 red shallots, thinly sliced

¾ cup peeled and diced cucumber

2 lime wedges

For the sauce:

3 red bird's-eye chiles

¼ cup rice vinegar

1 tablespoon water

Add the pork, jaggery, water, and dark and light soy sauces to a small saucepan. Simmer, uncovered, over medium heat for 30 to 40 minutes, stirring often, until the mixture has reduced in liquid and is dark and sticky. Add a dash or two more of water, if needed.

Set the rice to cook in a rice cooker or saucepan (see page 47). Meanwhile, swirl 1 tablespoon of the cooking oil around a wok on medium heat. Pour the beaten eggs into the wok and allow to set, flipping once. Remove the omelet from the wok, roll it up, slice it thinly, and set it aside.

Chop up the chiles for the sauce coarsely and add to the vinegar, along with the water. Let stand to marinate.

Wipe out the wok and heat up another tablespoon of cooking oil in it until just below smoking. Pat the dried shrimps dry and add to the oil. Stir-fry them for 30 seconds to 1 minute, and then set aside.

At this point, julienne the apple or peel and seed the green mango ready to serve so that it doesn't turn brown from hanging around too long.

By this stage, the rice should have cooked. Mix the shrimp paste into the rice, turning the rice over and over gently to mix in the paste evenly. It may take about 10 minutes, but you'll be left with brown-speckled rice.

To serve, lightly oil a rice bowl with the some of the remaining tablespoon of oil. Pack half of the rice into the bowl, and then turn it out onto a plate. Repeat with the other portion. Around the edge of each plate, arrange half the beans, shallots, omelet, cucumber, fried shrimps, and the apple or mango. Spoon a little of the sweet pork on top of the fried rice, and balance a wedge of lime on top. Serve with the chile vinegar sauce.

For me, miso is comforting, as well as soothing, and no more so than when it is coating a chunk of slow-cooked, wobbly pork belly. The Japanese believe miso has health-giving properties so, how better to treat such an ingredient than to flavor pork fat with it?

MISO-BRAISED PORK BELLY

Cut the pork belly into large cubes. Place in a saucepan of boiling water and boil for a couple of minutes; this is so that any scum comes floating to the surface now, and not in your stew.

Drain, rinse, and set the saucepan back on the heat. Put the oil and the onion in a layer on the bottom. You don't want them cooking much at the moment. Add the pork belly in a layer on top. Pour the sake evenly over the ingredients, and then the water. Cut a piece of nonstick parchment paper so that it fits into the pot nicely. Cover and cook on the lowest heat (you want a bare simmer) for 1½ hours.

Add the mirin, soy sauce, and sugar as well as the daikon. Cover, and cook for another hour. By now, the pork belly and the daikon should be tender; if not, cook a little longer. Discard the paper, then take out a ladleful of the stock. Stir it into the white and red miso until it dissolves, and then add it to the stew. Cook on the barest simmer for another 15 minutes—don't let it boil, because that will ruin any nutritional benefit in the miso.

Slice the white parts of the scallions and add to the stew. Julienne the green parts of the scallions and set aside for the garnish.

This isn't a thick stew (much of the liquid won't have evaporated), so it is best to serve it in a large bowl or a pasta dish. Serve over white rice, garnished with the julienned scallions.

SERVES 4 GREEDY PEOPLE OR 6 WITH OTHER DISHES

1 lb 9 oz boneless pork belly, skin on or off—if yours comes with ribs, simply remove them and use them for another dish, or for stock or congee (*see page 58*)

1 tablespoon cooking oil

1 white onion, finely sliced

¾ cup sake

3 cups water

1 tablespoon mirin

1½ tablespoons light soy sauce

2 teaspoons sugar

1 lb daikon (Asian radish), peeled and sliced into 1-inch thick disks

3 tablespoons white miso (*see page 16*)

2 teaspoons red miso (*see page 16*)

2 scallions, white and green parts separated

Although miso is a traditional Japanese ingredient, it also works well in sauces and butters. Its salty sweetness can be a little too strong for it to be used entirely on its own, but when combined with fats (in this case, mayonnaise and butter), it makes it not only easily spreadable, but gives it a more balanced flavor. You can make the Miso Mayo below from scratch, or alternatively stir miso paste into ready-made mayonnaise, tasting as you go for the desired strength of flavor.

SEARED SALMON & MISO MAYO SANDWICH

Pat the salmon dry, then dust with the chili powder and a little salt.

Add the oil and the salmon fillets, skin-side down, to a cold nonstick skillet. (This encourages the skin to crisp.) Turn the heat to medium and cook the salmon fillets for about 4 to 6 minutes, or until the skin has crisped. Turn the fillets over and cook for another minute, depending on the thickness.

Split each ciabatta open, toast the insides, and smear them with plenty of the miso mayo on both sides. Lay watercress on the bottom, along with the daikon, slightly overlapping in a fan shape. Place the salmon fillet on top, skin-side up, then top with the other half of the roll. Slice in half to serve.

2 salmon fillets, skin on—tail end is better, since they are flatter

chili powder, for dusting

salt

1 tablespoon cooking oil

2 single-serving ciabatta

1 quantity Miso Mayo (*see below*)

handful of watercress, chopped

Pickled Daikon (*see page 157*)

MISO MAYO

MAKES ENOUGH FOR SANDWICHES

pinch of salt

2 free-range egg yolks

1¾ cups peanut oil, divided

juice of ½ lemon

2½ tablespoons white miso (*see page 16*)

1 teaspoon Dijon mustard

Make sure the egg yolks, miso, and oil are all at room temperature before starting.

Add the salt to the egg yolks in a bowl and beat well by hand or using an electric beater. Add about half the oil in drops at first, making sure that each drop is incorporated, graduating to a very fine stream while beating the egg yolk mixture vigorously. I find it's far easier to rope in an unsuspecting roommate or partner to do the beating while you do the pouring. When the mixture becomes thick and a little lumpy, add the lemon juice, beating well. Once you've added half the oil, beat in 1 tablespoon of the miso and the mustard. Carry on beating in the oil in a slow stream until you have your desired consistency. Add the remaining miso and mix well to combine. If it becomes too thick, loosen it with a dash of water, little by little. This will keep for up to 3 days in a sterilized jar in the fridge.

1 tablespoon red miso (*see page 16*)

1½ tablespoons butter, soft but not liquefied

2 corn on the cob, freshly cooked (*see introduction*)

MISO-BUTTERED CORN ON THE COB

SERVES

2

There are several ways to cook corn on the cob. If you've got the weather for a barbecue, then there is no better method than cooking the cobs in their husks over indirect heat (though you need to soak the cobs in water first). At other times, cobs cooked in salted boiling water aren't a bad alternative.

Using a spoon, combine the miso with the butter in a bowl until it is well incorporated. Slather your just-cooked corn with it.

➽OTHER IDEAS

You can add what you like to the base butter recipe; a little garlic grated into the butter mixture, or shiso leaves, finely chopped, work nicely. I also like a little citrus, such as grated lemon or lime zest in the base butter with the juice squeezed over the cob. You can use the butter to flavor other vegetables, such as steamed broccoli or grilled asparagus, too, and it also works well on top of cooked meat, like steak, or fish. Add sesame seeds and a little vinegar, and replace the butter with peanut or olive oil for a salad dressing. What it definitely doesn't need is salt.

CHAPTER

RICE & NOODLES

Ask any Asian what one food they couldn't live without, and they might well say rice. If you held a gun to my head, I would probably say the same—I can't imagine life without those pearly white grains, steamed until fluffy, ready to receive any sauce you throw at them. The backbone of many an Asian meal, rice is a bland foil for the spread of dishes that a typical dinner will have, a necessity to loosen the flavors. It's associated with one of my earliest food memories—as a child, I trotted off to the rice cooker for a second helping and was sternly told off for not helping my elders to it first.

It is also a comfort; when I'm unwell, rice cooked for hours into a rice porridge called congee is life-giving. When I'm feeling lazy, a load of ingredients chucked in the rice cooker along with the rice all cook happily together into a one-pot meal. When my palate is jaded or I just can't be bothered, a spoonful of tomato ketchup stirred into a steaming bowl, eaten while watching TV does the trick; a stuck childhood memory of my best friend's Thai mother and her favorite snack.

Noodles, though. Where rice is the comfortable norm, noodles are the sexy little number. Egg noodles, rice noodles, bean thread noodles, mung bean noodles, sweet potato noodles, wheat noodles, fresh noodles, dried noodles ... the possibilities stretch before you endlessly. Much like pasta shapes, some noodles suit certain sauces better than others. Some have a texture that need a lighter dressing. Some can hold their own against heavy, rich sauces, while others are made to bathe or to be dunked into soups. Some simply look nicer in their appropriate preparation.

This chapter attempts to showcase the very best of rice and noodles in the kinds of dishes they're best suited to. This is by no means an exhaustive list (that could go on for reams), but rather the types most readily available to the Western consumer.

RICE

If you cook Asian food a lot, you really must buy a rice cooker. They are inexpensive, they cook rice perfectly and then keep it warm, and it's one less pan on the stove. Alternatively, you can cook rice in a saucepan with a tight-fitting lid (*see opposite*). Never salt the rice; the dishes that go with it are seasoned enough.

(1) GLUTINOUS (STICKY) RICE

Glutinous rice is a type of rice that becomes very sticky when cooked. The glutinous aspect doesn't pertain to gluten, but the way in which the rice behaves. When steamed, it becomes so dense you can pick up a whole clump all at once. It's often used in dim sum; the Cantonese wrap it in lotus leaves with flavorings like chicken and salted egg, before it is steamed. Always soak this rice overnight to reduce cooking time and improve texture. It's best steamed using the splatter screen and pan method (see below), or steamed within something.

(2) BLACK GLUTINOUS (STICKY) RICE

This is prepared in the same way as the white variety but more often used for sweet rather than savory dishes.

(3) SHORT-GRAIN RICE

Even though it is less sticky than its glutinous cousin, short-grain rice is still sticky enough to hold together. It is used seasoned with vinegar for sushi and commonly eaten with Japanese and Korean meals.

(4) LONG-GRAIN RICE

This includes fragrant jasmine and basmati rice, which has a distinct flavor and texture that I associate more with Indian food. More and more brown rice is being eaten nowadays, and you can opt for that if you like, but it doesn't have quite the sauce-mopping qualities that white rice does.

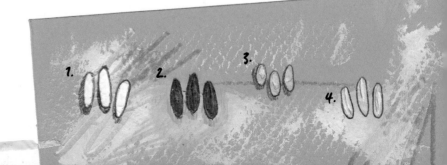

1.   2.   3.   4.

COOKING RICE WITHOUT A RICE COOKER

Rinse the grains well. Working to the ratio of 1 cup uncooked rice for 2 people, cook in 1¼ cups boiling water in a saucepan with a tight-fitting lid. Once the water boils, reduce the heat to low, place the lid on top, and simmer for 10 to 12 minutes. Once done, remove from the heat, fluff up the grains with a fork, and replace the lid to steam for another 10 minutes.

STEAMING GLUTINOUS (STICKY) RICE

Traditionally, the Thais cook glutinous rice using a large bamboo steamer. These are big contraptions and allow the rice to cook in steam instead of being submerged in water. Not many of us have the space for this at home, so an easier and far more popular method is to steam the rice using a splatter screen. These are metal disks with a wire screen and a handle that you place over skillets to stop oil from splattering out. You can buy these inexpensively and in various sizes; buy one bigger than a skillet you have that has a deep lip, or a saucepan.

To cook enough rice for two, soak 1 cup of glutinous (sticky) rice in water for 3 hours, then drain. Fill a saucepan or skillet halfway with boiling water, place the splatter screen over it, and add the rice in a pile in the middle. You should leave about 2 inches of air between the rice and the water. Bring the water to a gentle boil, then place a metal or heatproof plastic (glass or ceramic can be too heavy) mixing bowl over the rice and let steam for 30 minutes, turning the rice over once so that it does not get mushy. If you're cooking for a larger number of people, you may have to spread the rice out more and cook it for longer.

TOASTED GROUND RICE

This is essential for a lot of Thai salads, like larb, and dips, because of its nutty flavor and crunch. It also soaks up excess moisture in a dish, and sometimes binds it together. If a recipe calls for it, even just a little, it's always worth adding it for the flavor and texture profile it contributes. Glutinous (sticky) rice grains are best for this, since they break up more easily. To prepare, add the rice to a dry skillet over medium-low heat and, just as you would with pine nuts, toast them until they are golden brown but not burned. This will take at least 10 minutes, with regular stirring and shaking. Don't be tempted to use a higher heat—this will burn the grains.

Next, you can use a spice or coffee grinder or a mortar and pestle to finely grind the rice. The former gives a more uniform texture; the latter requires you to put in some elbow grease. Cover the top of the mortar and pestle and use a gentle pound-and-twist technique, otherwise your grains might ping off onto the kitchen floor before long. Grind to a fine powder and use to sprinkle on your dishes. You can keep the leftovers in an airtight container for a couple of weeks, but freshly ground really is best.

RICE NOODLES

A multitude of textures awaits you with noodles, all ready to be made into whatever you want. Rice noodles are defined by their width and shape and, in fact, many famous dishes are named after the shape of noodle used in them. My favorite of them all, ho fun, are wide, flat rice noodles most commonly bought fresh from the chilled foods section of the Asian supermarket. These are slippery and slithery in soups or loose sauces—a ruiner of white clothing—but are also substantial enough to take on the char and smoke of a wok in stir-fried dishes. Char kway teow, almost a national dish of Singapore and Malaysia, uses ho fun, and would be an entirely different and lesser dish without the glistening soft folds of these noodles.

(1) RICE VERMICELLI
(MEI FUN, BEEHOON OR BUN)

These are the thinnest, most delicate type of noodle. The equivalent of angel hair pasta, they are used for salads and stir-fries. You can use them in noodle soups too. Soak the noodles in hot water for 10 minutes, then drain well to use.

(2) KWAY CHAP (RICE FLAKES)

Shaped like big transparent squares or triangles, you soak these noodles in hot water for 10 minutes, drain them, and add them to richly spiced broths, such as in Kway Chap (*see page 64*). They work equally well in lighter broths, but can also be stir-fried. When cooked, they roll within themselves a little, trapping sauce inside, for a more substantial but still slippery and smooth mouthful.

(3) RICE STICKS
(FLAT RICE NOODLES OR PHO)

A wider variety of dried rice noodle, you soak them in boiling water for about 10 minutes until tender, drain them, and add them to noodle soups, at which point they become smooth and silky. Or you can stir-fry them, as in Pad Thai.

(4) JIANGXI (GUILIN, THICK RICE VERMICELLI, OR BUN)

Confusingly, the Vietnamese call any round rice noodle "bun," whatever the thickness. Almost as thick as spaghetti, these noodles are used in laksa (a rich, coconutty noodle soup), salads, and the famous "bun" noodle soups of Vietnam. They're always used fresh in Vietnam but, sadly, fresh bun are not easy to find elsewhere. Bun need to be cooked in boiling water for 3 to 7 minutes, depending on the brand. They have a wonderfully chewy texture.

EGG NOODLES

So-called egg and wheat noodles are slightly confusing because, while some are made with egg, others don't contain egg at all but are still called egg noodles because they look yellow. It's best to check the ingredients.

(5) ROUND EGG NOODLES (HOKKIEN)

You'll find these noodles in the chilled foods section, looking like a thicker, more vibrantly yellow spaghetti. Elastic and chewy, these noodles withstand being stir-fried very well and are ideal for rich, thick noodle soups. Refresh in boiling water to remove the excess oil, then proceed.

1.

2.

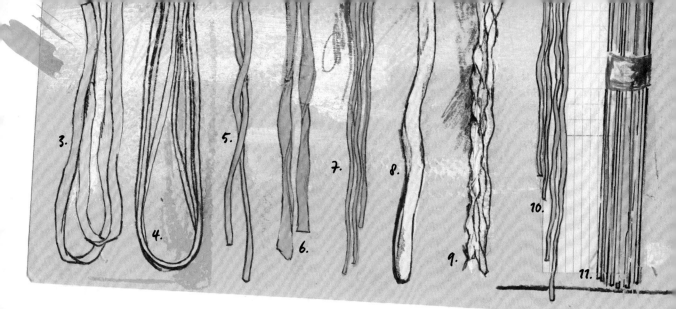

(6) FLAT EGG NOODLES

Sold dried in bundles, these are great tossed with a dressing, eaten cold in a salad, or stir-fried. Cook in simmering water for about 4 minutes, or until the bundle has relaxed, and then drain well and toss with a little cooking oil to prevent the noodles from sticking before using.

(7) HONG KONG NOODLES
(WONTON NOODLES OR LO MEIN)

Sold fresh in the chilled foods section, these are often tossed with a dressing (lo means "mix it up" and mein means "noodle," so refers to this method of preparation specifically) or used in noodle soups. Refresh in boiling water for 1 minute to remove some of the flour on the surface of the noodles, drain, and rinse with cold water. Then plunge them back into boiling water briefly to warm them before dressing. You can also buy these dried for convenience, and the top-quality versions contain shrimp roe (you will see tiny dots of it in each noodle strand). Cook the nests by simmering in boiling water for 3 to 5 minutes, then drain but keep the water the noodles were cooked in for dipping the noodles into or sipping on the side, since this water is flavored with the shrimp roe.

(8) SHANGHAI NOODLES & UDON

Shanghai noodles, usually found in the fridge section, are much like udon, which are Japanese wheat noodles. They are sometimes square and sometimes round and thicker than spaghetti, often prompting people to remark that they resemble worms. The most satisfying udon are the frozen or vacuum-packed varieties, but they are also sold dry. Heat through with boiling water until the udon cake has loosened, then drain and dress, add to noodle soups or stir-fry. Udon are eaten both hot in broth and cold with a dipping sauce, while Shanghai noodles are usually stir-fried and served hot.

(9 & 10) GLASS NOODLES (BEAN THREAD OR CELLOPHANE) & MUNG BEAN SHEET NOODLES

There are two main types of these noodles, made either with mung bean starch (9) or sweet potato starch (10). Both are used in braised dishes, salads, egg rolls, and soups, though the sweet potato variety, used more commonly in Korean cooking, is thicker and has a chewier texture. Smooth, slippery and jellylike, glass noodles get their name from their see-through quality. Mung bean sheets are noodles made from the same starch but in varying widths, and can sometimes come in sheets for you to break off as you see fit. Soak them in hot water for 10 to 30 minutes, depending on width, before using.

(11) SOBA (BUCKWHEAT) NOODLES

Soba noodles are always thin, and the Japanese eat them hot, cold, in soup, or with a dipping sauce. In Korea, they are almost always eaten cold in the summertime. Cook following the package instructions, then rinse and refresh in iced water.

E-FU (YI MEIN)

These round egg noodles are sold deep-fried into flat disks about the size of your palm. They have a spongy texture when cooked, and are often served at birthdays because the noodles, which are always long strands, symbolize a long life. These are most commonly eaten in restaurants, with luxurious ingredients, such as lobster and crab.

RAMEN

Chinese in origin, ramen noodles are now often thought of as synonymous with the Japanesse noodle soup dish. They are wheat noodles made with alkaline water to give them elasticity and come in thick or thin, wavy or straight varieties, depending on the type of ramen broth they're destined for. Instant noodles, since they mostly come in soup, are often called instant ramen.

Here, I've used glutinous rice, which clumps together once cooked, to stuff a chicken for a kind of alternative roast chicken with stuffing, if you will. The rice is flavored with all the chicken juices and is glistening with fat, compact, and rich. You only need a little to accompany your meat.

ROAST RICE-STUFFED CHICKEN

SERVES 4

Pound the whole garlic cloves with the piece of ginger in a mortar and pestle to a paste. Add the five-spice, vegetable oil, soy sauces, oyster sauce, and fermented bean curd and pound together into a sauce. Rub the mixture all over your chicken (reserving any left over), cover, and let marinate in the fridge overnight.

To cook, preheat the oven to 425°F. Heat the oil in a wok on medium heat, add the Chinese sausage, and fry until it changes color a little. Add the garlic and ginger, and then mix well. Add the mandarin peel to the wok along with the rice, and then stir in the rice wine and soy sauces. Cook for 5 minutes, turning the rice over and over again, until it is fairly dry. Stir in the scallions, remove from the heat, and let stand to cool completely.

Using a tablespoon, scoop the cooled rice into the cavity of the chicken, pushing it far down into the cavity to make room for more. Stuff until the cavity is full but not bursting. Tip the chicken up and carefully pour the water into the cavity, then place back down in a roasting pan. Roast for 20 minutes, then turn the oven down to 325°F and roast for another hour and 10 minutes, basting often. During the last 5 minutes, brush the chicken skin with the honey.

Skewer the thigh joint to check for doneness—the juices should run clear. Remove from the oven and let rest for 20 minutes before carving. Scoop a little rice out for each serving of chicken and spoon out a little of the juices from the bottom of the roasting pan to drizzle over each dish. Serve with garlicky greens.

3 garlic cloves, peeled
1-inch piece of fresh ginger root, peeled
½ teaspoon five-spice powder (*see page 205 for homemade*)
1 tablespoon vegetable oil
1 tablespoon dark soy sauce
2 tablespoons light soy sauce
3 tablespoons oyster sauce
1 cube of red fermented tofu (bean curd) (*see page 163*)
1 whole chicken, weighing about 3¼ lb
⅔ cup water
1 tablespoon liquid honey

For the rice

1 tablespoon cooking oil
2 Chinese sausages, thinly sliced
2 garlic cloves, minced
1 slice of fresh ginger root, peeled and minced
1 whole dried mandarin peel, soaked in just-boiled water for 10 minutes until soft, then drained and minced
1 cup glutinous (sticky) rice, soaked in cold water overnight, drained
3 tablespoons Shaoxing rice wine
2 tablespoons light soy sauce
1 teaspoon dark soy sauce
3 scallions, minced

This is the type of thing that Hong Kong's cuisine is famous for: A little bit Chinese, a little bit Westernized; slightly trashy but not regarded as so. This baked pork chop rice was a favorite of mine from Café de Coral in Hong Kong. Open for breakfast, lunch, and dinner, it's a fast-food restaurant chain, one my grandmother took me to frequently, so this is pure nostalgia for me. Along with this recipe is the standard method for egg-fried rice. You can embellish it to your heart's content to make a complete meal in itself.

HONG KONG-STYLE BAKED PORK CHOP RICE

SERVES 2

First, mix the rice wine and soy sauces together in a dish, add the pork chops, and turn them over to coat. Cover the dish with plastic wrap and let marinate in the fridge while you prepare the rest of the ingredients.

For the egg-fried rice, pour some boiling water over the peas to defrost them, then drain them. Heat the oil in a wok over high heat, swirling it to coat the sides, and add the rice, breaking up any clumps with your fingers. Cook the rice over the high heat until you see individual grains jumping—at that point they're ready to be stirred. Stir the peas into the rice, then move the mixture to one side of the wok. Crack both eggs into the wok and add the soy sauce. Stir-fry briskly for 30 seconds, then remove from the heat and add the sliced scallion. Transfer the rice to a baking dish, or 2 individual dishes that can go in the oven.

Preheat the oven to 425°F. Heat the oil for the sauce in a saucepan, add the onion, garlic, and tomatoes and cook over medium heat, or until the tomatoes are starting to break down a little, the onion is translucent, and the garlic is fragrant. Add the ketchup, Worcestershire sauce, sugar, salt, and water, then simmer gently for 10 to 15 minutes. Mix the cornstarch with a little cold water until smooth, stir it into the pan, and cook until thickened. Then remove from the heat.

While the sauce is simmering, heat the remaining 2 tablespoons of oil in a nonstick skillet. Shake the marinade off of the pork chops and dust with cornstarch, then fry them in the hot oil over medium heat for 5 minutes on each side until cooked. Let rest for 5 minutes and then slice.

Top the rice with the pork, then pour the sauce evenly over the pork slices. Scatter the 2 cheeses on top and bake for 15 minutes so that the cheese has melted and everything is bubbling.

1 tablespoon Shaoxing rice wine
1 tablespoon light soy sauce
1 teaspoon dark soy sauce
2 pork chops off the bone, fat scored (this prevents them from curling up)
2 tablespoons cooking oil
cornstarch, for dusting

For the egg-fried rice:
1/3 cup frozen peas
2 tablespoons cooking oil
1½ cups cooked (preferably the day before) and cooled fragrant jasmine rice
2 free-range eggs
1 teaspoon light soy sauce
1 scallion, diagonally sliced

For the sauce:
1 tablespoon cooking oil
½ white onion, coarsely chopped
2 garlic cloves, minced
3 tomatoes, coarsely diced
1/3 cup tomato ketchup
1 tablespoon Worcestershire sauce
1 teaspoon sugar
pinch of salt
½ cup water
1 teaspoon cornstarch
handful of shredded mozzarella cheese
handful of shredded sharp Cheddar cheese

My parents used to make me this soup for breakfast once a month or so, whenever we had rice left over from a weekend dinner. It is everything I love in a breakfast; hot, nourishing, and with bright and sparky flavors. The condiments are served on the side for you to help yourself, so that every bite and every slurp of soup can be customized—you'll need a few saucers for these. There is, of course, nothing quite like chile and garlic to wake up to, and these days I find it's a pretty wonderful hangover cure.

THAI RICE SOUP

Add the stock, celery, and ginger to a large saucepan over medium heat. Chop the lemon grass stalk in half and add to the pot with the rice. Bring the stock to a simmer. Mix the ground chicken with the salt and white pepper, roll into small balls, and drop carefully into the soup. Simmer gently on low heat for 15 to 20 minutes, or until cooked through.

Meanwhile, chop the cilantro finely and place in a saucer for people to add to their bowls.

Pour the fish sauce into another saucer or small serving bowl. Mince the chiles and scatter them into the fish sauce.

Peel and then smash up the garlic clove using a mortar and pestle, or crush it, mix it with the lime juice, and place in another saucer. Put the saucers on the table for people to help themselves.

2 pints chicken stock
1 celery stalk, diced
2 slices of fresh ginger root, peeled
1 lemon grass stalk
1¾ cups cold leftover cooked rice
7 oz ground chicken
pinch of salt
pinch of ground white pepper
bunch of fresh cilantro
¼ cup fish sauce
3 bird's-eye chiles (fewer, if you are feeling very hung over)
1 garlic clove
juice of 3 limes

The Koreans and the Chinese both eat rice cakes, though in different shapes. The latter eat oval-shaped cakes, often found dried, usually around Chinese New Year for good fortune, while the Korean version is tube- or pillow-shaped and eaten far more frequently. Rice cakes are filling but they don't taste of anything, so are usually cooked with strong flavors; tteokbokki is a popular Korean street food and consists of rice cakes cooked with gochujang, which this recipe is based on. Here, I've added a couple of Western ingredients for maximum flavor.

KOREAN RICE CAKES with CHORIZO and GREENS

SERVES 4

If your rice cakes are dried, soak them in water for 24 hours before use. Bring a large saucepan of water to a boil, add the rice cakes, and simmer for 3 minutes. Then rinse in cold water, drain, and place in a bowl. Add the sesame oil and toss to coat.

Heat up a wok, add the cooking chorizo, and fry it gently to release the oils. If it's looking dry, add the tablespoon of cooking oil. Add the yellow onion and fry gently until softened. Add the kimchi, garlic, and gochujang, and fry well for a few minutes. Then add the rice wine and the kale or cavolo nero. Fry gently for another 10 minutes, or until the kale or cabbage is tender. Add the rice cakes, sugar, and the stock or water and simmer over low heat for a few more minutes. The dish will thicken with the addition of the rice cakes.

Remove from the heat, stir in the scallions and cilantro, and serve immediately.

14 oz bag frozen rice cakes, in pillow shapes or dried disks (see above)

1 tablespoon sesame oil

3 small hot chorizo cooking sausages, skinned and coarsely chopped

1 tablespoon cooking oil (optional)

1 yellow onion, sliced into thin half-moons

3 tablespoons cabbage kimchi (see page 143 for homemade), coarsely chopped

2 garlic cloves, minced

1½ tablespoons gochujang (see page 16)

2 tablespoons Shaoxing rice wine

2 handfuls of kale or cavolo nero, coarsely chopped

1 teaspoon superfine sugar

²/₃ cup chicken stock or water

2 scallions, diagonally sliced

small handful of fresh cilantro leaves, coarsely chopped

3 pandan leaves, tied in a knot, or **1 teaspoon** vanilla extract

½ cup black glutinous (sticky) rice, soaked in cold water overnight and drained

3 tablespoons desiccated coconut

⅓ cup jaggery (palm sugar)

1 large ripe mango

⅔ cup coconut milk

3 tablespoons pomegranate seeds

BLACK STICKY RICE *with* MANGO

SERVES 4

The traditional Thai dessert is sticky rice with mango made with white glutinous rice, but this works equally well. The black glutinous rice makes a dramatic dish, especially when enhanced by the colorful vibrancy of the fruit. You can turn this into a breakfast or brunch dish by adding sunflower seeds, pumpkin seeds, and orange segments. Experiment with different kinds of fruit, such as strawberries, dragonfruit, or blueberries.

Bring 2 cups of water to a boil in a large saucepan and add the pandan leaves or the vanilla extract. Add the rice and simmer, uncovered, for 40 minutes on medium heat, stirring every 10 minutes, until the grains are soft and most of the water is absorbed. Some grains may have split, which is OK. Stir well and set to one side. If it's looking very wet, drain off the water.

Meanwhile, toast the desiccated coconut in a dry nonstick skillet on the lowest heat, stirring often, for 10 minutes, or until the coconut is golden brown and crumbly. Add the toasted coconut to a food processor or spice or coffee grinder and grind it until it is a fine texture.

Add 1 cup of water to a small saucepan over medium heat. Stir in the palm sugar and continue stirring until it has dissolved. Let the mixture simmer for 5 minutes, or until it has reached the consistency of a rich syrup. Then remove from the heat and stir into the cooked rice.

Peel the mango skin away from the flesh and, using a sharp knife, cut the mango flesh into wedges from either side of the seed. Warm the coconut milk briefly in a small saucepan. To serve, divide the rice among 4 individual bowls and drizzle each one with the coconut milk. Place a few mango wedges on the side, then scatter with the pomegranate seeds. Finally, sprinkle with a pinch or two of the toasted ground coconut.

I'm willing to beg that every Asian country has a variant of congee, a type of porridge. It is made by cooking rice in a lot of water or stock until it breaks down to varying thicknesses, depending on which country you're from or what your preference is. The Cantonese (who call it jook) often favor a thick, wallpaper paste-like soup that is creamy and without much differentiation in grains, while Teochew style is thinner, with the rice grains kept intact. It's usually a breakfast food, and often food for the infirm, the elderly, and the young. The key to a good congee is either cooking it with lots of flavor (such as in stock made from chicken carcasses or pork bones), or serving it with lots of tasty things to add to it.

CONGEE

Wash the rice a couple of times, then drain. Add the rice to a saucepan with the water and bring to a boil. Simmer gently, partially covered, on low heat for an hour, stirring a few times. If you like this consistency, remove from the heat. If you prefer a thicker, creamier style, cook for longer, stirring more often, until it has reached your desired consistency. If it becomes too thick, you can loosen it with a little water.

½ cup fragrant jasmine rice

3¾ cups water

SERVES 2

SUGGESTED ADDITIONS

Sometimes I eat congee for sustenance when I'm under the weather, in which case I prefer plain congee. Other times, when I want a full meal, I add one of the following:

Fish fillets or slices of pork loin (1), marinated in a little soy sauce and cornstarch and then cooked by swishing in the congee for 5 minutes until just cooked through.

Ground chicken (2), seasoned with white pepper, formed into balls, and dropped into the congee to cook for 5 minutes.

Salted egg yolk (*see page 163*), steamed for 3 minutes and finely chopped.

POPULAR TOPPINGS

Nori (3) (*see page 188*), toasted under the broiler until crisp, and then crumbled into flakes.

Pork cracklings (4)—yup, just bash them up a little and throw them in. Some go a little soggy and soft, while others retain crispiness; I love the contrast.

Scallion (5).

Fresh cilantro. (6)

Fresh ginger root (7), cut into matchsticks and sizzled in 1 tablespoon hot cooking oil.

Fish skin chips (8).

Roasted peanuts (9).

Century egg (10) (*see page 163*), shelled and diced.

Toasted sesame seeds (11).

Preserved vegetable omelet (12), cooked with a splash of fish sauce and Tianjin preserved vegetable (*see page 162*).

Pickled vegetables—spicy pickled turnip, pickled mustard green (*see page 162*).

Egg yolk, dropped into a bowl of piping hot congee (the yolk will cook in the residual heat).

Poached egg.

Deep-fried dough stick—in Hong Kong and Taiwan, these savory doughnuts are dipped into congee or soymilk. Heavenly.

I miss Malaysia. My trip there in April 2011 affected me greatly; it was one of the most hard-core eating trips I've done. After day three I forgot how it felt to be hungry and instead felt only "full," "really very full," and "ohmygod-I'm-gonna-barf." The ease of getting a quick bowl of noodles for next to nothing made me giddy and I hit the noodle soups hard, one of my favorites being Curry Mee. This thick, spicy, and coconutty soup contained chunks of congealed pig's blood and little cockles, as well as tofu puffs and shrimp. Alas, it's not as easy to get hold of pig's blood and cockles back home, so my version leaves these out (you may be relieved to hear).

MALAYSIAN CURRY MEE

14 fl oz can coconut milk

1 cup chicken stock

4 fresh kaffir lime leaves

branch of fresh curry leaves

6 tofu puffs (*see page 128*), halved

3½ oz fish cake (*see page 129*), thinly sliced

2 free-range eggs

handful of green snap beans

handful of bean sprouts

10½ oz fresh yellow egg noodles

3½ oz dried rice vermicelli, cooked and cooled

For the curry paste:

15 small purple shallots

7 garlic cloves

3-inch piece of fresh ginger root, peeled

6 dried red chiles, soaked in just-boiled water for about 30 minutes until soft and then drained

4 lemon grass stalks, tender inner parts only

roots or stems of a bunch of fresh cilantro

2 teaspoons ground coriander

1 teaspoon belacan (shrimp paste) (*see page 17*)

1 teaspoon sugar

vegetable oil, for blending and storing

To serve:

handful of fresh cilantro

1 lime, quartered

sambal oelek

Chop all the paste ingredients coarsely and then blend in a mini food processor or a blender, adding some oil as you go to make a fine paste. Any leftover paste should be kept in a sterilized airtight jar with a film of oil on top in the fridge (it will keep for a week).

In a large saucepan, slowly fry 2 tablespoons curry paste per person, so 8 tablespoons in this instance, for 15 minutes. Add the coconut milk, the stock, lime leaves, and curry leaf branch (keeping the leaves on the branch makes them easier to remove later). Cover and let simmer gently for 35 minutes. Add the tofu puffs for the last 15 minutes and the fish cake slices for the last 5, then remove the pan from the heat. Remove and discard the curry leaf branch.

Add the eggs to a saucepan of boiling water and cook for 6 minutes, then remove from the heat, drain, and hold them under cold running water to cool. Peel carefully.

In another saucepan of boiling water, simmer the green snap beans for 3 minutes, adding the bean sprouts to blanch for the final 30 seconds, and then drain. Cook the egg noodles following the package instructions (mine required just plunging into boiling water for a couple of minutes) and drain.

To serve, divide the egg noodles and vermicelli noodles equally among 4 deep bowls. Top with the bean sprouts and green beans. Heat up the soup base until simmering, then distribute equally between the bowls. Halve each egg over the bowls and carefully place an egg half in each. Scatter with the cilantro and serve with one lime quarter per bowl, along with the sambal oelek.

Served cold, these noodles are warming, hearty, and filling, the very antithesis of a limp, cold noodle salad. In a pinch you can use tahini in place of the dark sesame paste (*see page 17*), but you won't get as rich a flavor. You can, however, use virtually any crunchy sliced vegetable; I've made this with blanched broccoli, green snap beans, and even red cabbage. When I'm trying to eat lighter, I up the vegetables and down the noodles, and it makes a great packed lunch with grilled chicken or salmon.

SESAME & PEANUT NOODLE SALAD

SERVES 4 AS A SIDE DISH

2 **tablespoons** unsalted raw peanuts

1 **tablespoon** white sesame seeds

1 large carrot, peeled and julienned

1 red bell pepper, cored, seeded, and thinly sliced into strips

handful of sugar snap peas, thinly sliced vertically

handful of bean sprouts

2 scallions, greens parts only, julienned

2 **nests (about 7 oz)** of flat dried egg noodles

a few stalks of fresh cilantro, coarsely chopped, to garnish

For the dressing:

2 **tablespoons** chunky peanut butter

3 **tablespoons** dark sesame paste (see recipe introduction)

1 **tablespoon** sesame oil

1 **tablespoon** chili oil

2 **tablespoons** light soy sauce

2 **tablespoons** warm water

1½ **tablespoons** rice vinegar

1 **teaspoon** superfine sugar

1-inch piece of fresh ginger root, peeled and minced

1 large red chile, minced

For the dressing, mix the peanut butter with the sesame paste, oils, soy sauce, warm water, and vinegar. Add the sugar, ginger, and chile and mix thoroughly so that it becomes emulsified. This is easiest to do in a clean, empty jar with a tight-fitting lid; secure the lid and shake well.

Add the peanuts to a dry skillet on medium heat and toast for several minutes until golden but not burned, shaking the pan every so often. Remove and let cool, then chop coarsely. Add the sesame seeds to the skillet and toast until fragrant, shaking the pan often.

Add all your vegetables to a large bowl. Cook the egg noodles following the package instructions and then drain and refresh under cold water so they stop cooking and don't stick together. Drain really well, and then add to the vegetables. Add the dressing and get your hands in there, working the dressing into the mixture throughout. Garnish with the cilantro and the toasted peanuts and sesame seeds.

This wouldn't be classed as one of the world's best-looking dishes, but mention it to any Chinese, Singaporean or Malaysian and a misty-eyed expression of homesickness will take over their faces. Ho fun noodles are essential for this—no other will do for that ultimate comfort of springy, satisfying rice noodles in a soothing, thick gravy.

SEAFOOD HO FUN IN EGG GRAVY

SERVES 2 TO 3

Soak the ho fun in a bowl of hot water, separating the noodle strands carefully with your fingers. Drain, add to a bowl with the dark soy sauce, and toss to coat.

Heat 1 tablespoon of the cooking oil in a wok on medium heat until it is shimmering. Add half the garlic and the noodles and stir-fry over high heat to get some caramelization on the noodles for a couple of minutes. Transfer to a serving dish and let stand in a warm place.

Bring a saucepan of water to a boil. Blanch the greens in the boiling water for 2 minutes and remove with a slotted spoon. Blanch the squid, shrimp, and the fish cake or balls for 2 minutes, then remove and place on top of the noodles with the greens.

Wipe the wok clean. Put back on medium heat, add the remaining tablespoon of oil and fry the remaining garlic, the ginger, and bacon together for 2 to 3 minutes. Add the stock, light soy sauce, white pepper, oyster sauce, and sugar. Simmer for 3 minutes, then add the cornstarch solution and cook until it has thickened to a consistency like gravy.

Turn the heat off and drizzle the beaten egg in, stirring as you go, so that you get strands of egg suspended in the sauce. Pour evenly over the noodles and serve immediately, garnished with the scallion.

13 oz package fresh ho fun noodles (*see page 48*)

1 tablespoon dark soy sauce

2 tablespoons cooking oil, divided

4 garlic cloves, minced, divided

a few leaves of choy sum or other leafy green vegetable

1 small squid, cleaned and sliced into rings

10 uncooked peeled jumbo shrimp

½ fish cake, thinly sliced, or 6 fish balls, halved (*see page 129*)

1 teaspoon peeled and grated fresh ginger root

2 strips unsmoked bacon, finely chopped

2 cups chicken stock

1½ tablespoons light soy sauce

pinch of ground white pepper

1 tablespoon oyster sauce

pinch of superfine sugar

3 tablespoons cornstarch, mixed with **3 tablespoons** cold water

2 free-range eggs, beaten

1 scallion, minced

Kway chap is the name of this Singaporean dish but also of the shape of the noodle. When dried, they are triangular-shaped flakes, but once you cook them, they become soft and often roll into a cigar shape, trapping the intensely spiced broth of this recipe within its folds. Traditionally, all sorts of piggy offal is simmered in the broth, too. However, since that's not entirely easy to find and also somewhat challenging, I've left it out.

6 KWAY CHAP

1 fresh pork shank

1 **tablespoon** cooking oil

6 star anise

3-inch piece of fresh ginger root, peeled and bashed with the flat side of a knife

3 garlic cloves, lightly crushed

3 cinnamon sticks

5 cloves

1 bay leaf

1 black cardamom

¼ **cup** light soy sauce

1 **tablespoon** dark soy sauce

1 **tablespoon** sugar

3 free-range eggs

8 tofu puffs (see page 128)

14 oz dried rice flake noodles

2 **tablespoons** Chinkiang black vinegar

¼ oz Chinese rock sugar

For the chile & ginger sauce:
10 large red chiles

2-inch piece of fresh ginger root, peeled and coarsely chopped

pinch of salt

1 **teaspoon** water

Blanch the pork shank in a saucepan of boiling water for 3 minutes, and then drain and rinse. Clean out the inside of the pan—this is so that you won't have to skim any scum off of the broth.

Heat the oil in a large saucepan over medium heat and fry the star anise, ginger, garlic, cinnamon sticks, cloves, and bay leaf for 2 minutes, stirring constantly. Add the pork shank and black cardamom, and then add the light soy sauce, dark soy sauce, and sugar. Pour enough water into the saucepan to cover the pork, and turn the heat up to high. Once boiling, turn the heat down to low and cover. Simmer very gently for 2 hours.

Meanwhile, cook the eggs in a saucepan of simmering water for 7 minutes. Drain the eggs and hold them under cold running water to cool, and then shell them. Soak the tofu puffs in just-boiled water for 10 minutes. Then squeeze the water out of them and chop each one in half.

Add the eggs and tofu puffs to the pan and simmer for another 30 minutes.

To make the chile and ginger sauce to accompany the meal, seed the chiles and chop coarsely. Add to a blender along with the ginger, salt, and water and blend until smooth. Transfer to a serving bowl.

Bring a large saucepan of water to a boil. Add the rice flakes and cook for 5 to 8 minutes, or until soft. Drain and divide them among serving bowls.

To serve, lift the pork shank out of the broth and place on a platter. Fish out the eggs and halve them, arranging them around the pork, then do the same with the tofu puffs. Flavor the broth with the Chinkiang vinegar and Chinese rock sugar, stirring over low heat to dissolve, then ladle the spiced broth into the bowls with the noodles, avoiding the large spices. Serve the platter of meat with the chile and ginger sauce for people to dip into.

This salad is everything I love about Thai food. Pretty on the plate, the flavors of the herbs make it refreshing and bright, and the lemon grass and lime leaves have an unparalleled fragrance. The noodles are slippery, but the ground pork and vegetables get caught up in their glassy tangles. It's not for the faint-hearted, so dial it down or seed the chiles if you're feeding those of a delicate constitution. I make big batches of this for picnics or barbecues, since it works incredibly well cold or at room temperature.

THAI GLASS NOODLE
SALAD (YUM WOON SEN)

SERVES 4 AS A SIDE

If you're using mung bean noodles, let the noodles soak in hot (not boiling) water for 10 minutes, or until tender. If you're using sweet potato noodles (which are a bit more robust), boil enough water to cover the noodles in a bowl, then let them soak for 15 minutes, or until tender.

Toast the peanuts and cashews in a dry skillet over low heat for about 10 minutes, or until golden, shaking the pan every so often so that they don't burn. Set aside.

Slice the red onion into half-moons and place in a bowl with the pinch of salt and the juice of 1 lime. Let soak for at least 15 minutes while you prepare the rest of the salad—this removes the harshness of the raw onion.

Drain the dried shrimps and pound using a mortar and pestle for 10 minutes, or until they have broken down into a mush. Chop the bird's-eye chiles finely, then add to the shrimp, pounding a few times to amalgamate it. Add the sugar, fish sauce, and the juice of the remaining lime, combining as you go. Taste the dressing—is it sour enough, sweet enough, savory enough?—and adjust if necessary.

Add the celery and red bell pepper to a large bowl. Drain the noodles and rinse with cold water, then drain thoroughly and add to the bowl. Add the mint and cilantro, tossing well so that everything is evenly distributed. Drain the red onions and rinse them, then add them, too.

Heat the oil in a skillet or wok over high heat and fry the ground pork, breaking up any lumps. Add the lemon grass and sliced lime leaves and stir-fry until the pork takes on some color. Add the shrimp and stir-fry for a little longer until they are completely pink. Remove from the heat and add to the bowl of noodles. Pour in the dressing and carefully toss together, using your hands once the pork has cooled a little. Finally, bash up the nuts using the mortar and pestle, and garnish the salad with them.

7 oz dried mung bean or sweet potato glass noodles (see page 49)

2 tablespoons unsalted peanuts

2 tablespoons unsalted cashews

1 small red onion

pinch of salt

juice of 2 limes, divided

2 tablespoons dried shrimps, washed and soaked in just-boiled water for 10 minutes

2 red bird's-eye chiles

2 teaspoons sugar

¼ cup fish sauce

1 celery stalk, peeled and julienned

1 red bell pepper, cored, seeded, and julienned

3 sprigs of mint, leaves removed and coarsely chopped

small handful of fresh cilantro, coarsely chopped

1 teaspoon cooking oil

9 oz ground pork

1 lemon grass stalk, woody outer layers discarded, and tender inner parts minced

3 kaffir lime leaves, rolled up and thinly sliced

10 large, raw peeled shrimp

It's not often I favor chicken over pork, but having tried this recipe in both guises, the lighter flavor of the chicken actually works better and complements the pickled vegetables perfectly. Don't get me wrong—chicken will never steal my heart as pork does (I am part Chinese, after all), but pork is somehow too flavorsome here. This is a favorite of mine when I'm feeling under the weather; the silky slippery noodles are comforting, while the spicy sour flavors feel like they're doing battle in your body against whatever ails you.

HOT *and* SOUR CHICKEN NOODLES

SERVES
2

Soak the sweet potato noodles in boiling water following the package instructions until cooked. Meanwhile, skin and debone the chicken thighs. Put into a food processor with the ginger and pulse until coarsely ground.

Rinse the pickled vegetable and set to one side. Heat the cooking oil in a wok over high heat, add the garlic, chicken mixture, and the chiles and stir-fry until there is no pink left in the meat. Add the chili bean paste and stir-fry until everything is coated. Throw in the pickled vegetable, soy sauce, vinegar, sugar, and stock, and simmer for 10 minutes. Meanwhile, steam your vegetables for serving.

To assemble, place the noodles in the bowl and top with the vegetables. Set the chicken mixture on top with half the broth per bowl. Finally, drizzle the sesame oil on top of each serving and garnish with the scallions.

5½ oz dried sweet potato glass noodles (*see page 49*)

2 chicken thighs

1-inch piece of fresh ginger root, peeled and coarsely chopped

1 oz sachet of ready-sliced Sichuan zha cai (*see page 162*), or any kind of pickled vegetable will do

1 tablespoon cooking oil

3 garlic cloves, minced

2 long red chiles, minced

2 tablespoons chili bean paste (*see page 16*)

1 tablespoon light soy sauce

1 tablespoon Chinkiang black vinegar

1 teaspoon sugar

1¼ cups chicken stock

steamed bok choy, or any greens of your choice really (I used bok choy and sugar snap peas), to serve

1 teaspoon sesame oil

2 scallions, diagonally sliced, to garnish

In Japanese, yaki means fried, and udon is a thick wheat noodle that stands up incredibly well to being fried at high heat, thanks to its robust nature and satisfying chew. You can really use anything you have lying around for this recipe; when I'm down to odds and ends of vegetables left lying in the fridge, more often than not they will be sliced up and stir-fried in this manner. It's a filling and quick dish, and a staple for busy weekdays when I don't have much time to cook.

YAKI UDON

SERVES 1

7 oz vacuum-packed or frozen udon

1 tablespoon cooking oil

2 garlic cloves, minced

½ small white onion, thinly sliced into half-moons

2 stalks of green sprouting broccoli

1 small carrot, peeled and julienned

3½ oz boneless, skinless chicken breast, thinly sliced, or raw peeled shrimp

handful of bean sprouts

1 Chinese or white cabbage leaf, rolled up and thinly sliced

1 tablespoon mirin

1 tablespoon light soy sauce

1 teaspoon pickled ginger, julienned (optional)

1 scallion, green part only, diagonally sliced

1 tablespoon dried bonito flakes (*see page 209*)

For vacuum-packed noodles, run them under warm water to loosen. If the noodles are frozen, soak them in boiling water until the strands loosen and then drain.

Heat the oil in a wok over high heat. Add the noodles and garlic, followed by the onion, broccoli, carrot, and chicken or shrimp, and stir-fry briskly for 2 to 3 minutes. Add the bean sprouts, followed by the cabbage, and stir-fry for 2 minutes. Then add the mirin and soy sauce and stir-fry for another minute.

Spoon out into a bowl or plate, topping the noodles with the scallion greens and the pickled ginger. Scatter with the bonito flakes to serve.

Traditionally, char siu (Cantonese roast pork) is made using pork tenderloin. But I find that fat is flavor when it comes to meat, so I much prefer to use shoulder. An inexpensive cut, it is interspersed with fat, which keeps it moist. These noodles need barely any cooking at all, since they're quite thin. A plunge in boiling water and a rinse in cold water to get rid of the starch and then a warmup is all they really require to keep that essential bite and elasticity.

DRY-TOSSED CHAR SIU NOODLES

SERVES 2

1 lb 2 oz boneless pork shoulder steaks, cut into strips

2 tablespoons liquid honey

2 bundles of fresh wonton or Hong Kong noodles

For the marinade:

4 garlic cloves

large slice of fresh ginger root, peeled

2 tablespoons hoi sin sauce

1 tablespoon yellow bean paste (*see page 16*)

½ teaspoon DIY Five-spice Powder (*see page 205 for homemade*)

1 teaspoon sesame oil

1 teaspoon Shaoxing rice wine

For the sauce:

¾ cup scallion slices

1½ oz fresh ginger root

pinch of salt

1 tablespoon cooking oil

1 tablespoon sesame oil

2 tablespoons light soy sauce

1 tablespoon oyster sauce

1 teaspoon rice vinegar

Mix the marinade ingredients together in a bowl. Add the pork shoulder strips and stir to coat them in the mixture. Cover the dish with plastic wrap and let marinate in the fridge overnight.

An hour or so before you are ready to cook the pork, remove it from the fridge and let it stand to come up to room temperature. Meanwhile, preheat the oven to 400°F. Place the pork strips on a rack set into a roasting pan and roast for 40 minutes, turning them once halfway through the cooking time. Decant the juices from the roasting pan and mix with the honey. Brush the pork shoulder strips with this and roast for another 5 minutes. Remove from the oven and let rest in a warm place for 15 minutes.

Meanwhile, for the sauce, slice the scallion finely, and peel and mince the ginger. Place in a bowl with the rest of the sauce ingredients. Stir well to combine and set aside for at least 10 minutes so that all the flavors have time to blend.

Bring a large saucepan of water to a boil, and put a colander in the sink. Place the bundles of noodles in the boiling water for 30 seconds, then transfer to the colander with a slotted spoon, reserving the boiling water. Wash the noodles under cold water—this gets rid of the excess starch on the noodles. Just before serving, plunge the noodles back into the hot water for another 30 seconds before draining and tossing with the ginger and scallion sauce. Chop the char siu and serve on top of the noodles.

4 strips of bacon, chopped into small pieces

½ sheet of nori (*see page 188*), toasted under the grill until crisp

1 small head of purple sprouting broccoli or any other dark leafy green

1 scallion

1 fat garlic clove

2 handfuls of shredded Parmesan cheese

2 free-range egg yolks

2 x 7 oz blocks of vacuum-packed or frozen udon

freshly ground black pepper

UDON CARBONARA

SERVES **2**

This is an enormous bastardization of the classic Italian carbonara. Traditionalists will wince, Italians might issue death threats, but I am pushing on with—dare I say it—fusion. Udon is the perfect noodle for this; thick, wormlike, chewy and slippery; it is much more satisfying than spaghetti. The creamy, cheesy sauce clings to each strand like a sexy hug. I've Asian-ed it with the addition of scallion and toasted nori, the latter of which adds another whack to an already umami-packed dish.

Fry the bacon in a nonstick skillet over medium heat until most of the fat has rendered and the bacon is starting to get crisp.

While the bacon is frying, crush the nori in your hands into a bowl so that it becomes large flakes/dust. Separate the broccoli into small florets, trimming away any tough parts. Separate the white part of the scallion and shred finely. Mince the green part and reserve for the garnish.

Crush the garlic, add to the bacon in the skillet, and fry gently on low heat for a couple of minutes. Add the whites of the scallion, then immediately remove from the heat.

Whisk the Parmesan with the egg yolks in a large bowl. Bring a saucepan of water to a boil and cook the broccoli or leafy greens for 1 minute, then add the udon and cook following the package instructions (usually about 3 minutes, or until the blocks have loosened and untangled). Reserve ¼ cup of the cooking water, then drain the noodles well and add to the egg and cheese mixture. Add the bacon mixture and toss well with the reserved cooking water. The egg and Parmesan mixture will emulsify into a sauce, coating the udon strands as you keep tossing. Garnish with the scallion greens, toasted nori, and plenty of black pepper. Serve immediately on warmed plates.

A cold noodle soup, especially an icy, sour one, might be an alien concept that takes getting used to, but it's perfect for a hot summer's day. The buckwheat noodles in this preparation are chewy and elastic, giving you a proper pull from the bowl.

KOREAN SUMMERTIME NOODLES (MUL NAENGMYEON)

Rinse the beef brisket under cold running water. Bring the water to a boil in a large saucepan with the anchovies, shiitake mushrooms, and kombu. Boil on high heat for 15 minutes, and then add the beef brisket. Cover and let simmer on low heat for 40 minutes.

Remove the beef and set aside. Drain the stock through a fine sieve into a large bowl. Discard the kombu, anchovies, and mushrooms. Season the broth with the salt, sugar, and vinegar, then taste—it should be quite tangy. Let cool and then place in the freezer for a minimum of 30 minutes, but a maximum of 1 hour—it should be a slushy liquid when serving, not solid.

Bring a large saucepan of water to a boil, add the noodles, and cook for 3 to 5 minutes, or following the package instructions. Drain well and then plunge into cold water. Drain again, and plunge back into fresh cold water.

Slice the halves from the pear either side of the core, then cut them into thin slices. Slice the beef brisket as thinly as you can, and slice the cucumber into thin half-moons.

To assemble the noodles, pour half the cold broth into each of 2 serving bowls. Add a tangle of noodles and top with a few slices of the brisket. Top with 3 slices of the pear and a few of the cucumber half-moons, followed by a hard-cooked egg half. Scatter this with the scallion greens. Set a pile of kimchi on top of the noodles to the side and sprinkle each bowl with the toasted sesame seeds. Smear half a teaspoon of English mustard onto the inside lip of each bowl so that the eater can dab as they see fit.

5½ oz beef brisket
3 cups water
8 dried anchovies, heads pinched off
2 dried shiitake mushrooms
piece of dried kombu (*see page 188*), about 3 x 5in in size
½ teaspoon salt
pinch of sugar
1 tablespoon rice vinegar
9 oz Korean buckwheat noodles
1 Asian pear
1 small cucumber
1 free-range hard-cooked egg, shelled and halved
1 scallion, green part only, julienned
2 tablespoons radish kimchi (chong gak) or cabbage kimchi (*see page 143 for homemade*)
1 tablespoon white sesame seeds, toasted
1 teaspoon English mustard

01 Combine the noodles, lettuce, carrot, and cilantro in a bowl and mix together well.

Mix the sauce ingredients together in a suitable bowl until well combined.

Prepare a bowl of hand-hot water. Lay out a clean, dry dish towel in front of you.

Dip a wrapper in the water and leave it there for a few seconds—it should start softening up. Remove from the water and lay out flat on the dish towel.

Add about 2 tablespoons of the filling to the center of the wrapper, but slightly nearer the bottom closest to you. Top with a tablespoon of crab or pork etc., (if using).

VIETNAMESE SUMMER ROLLS

Rice paper is the Vietnamese version of an egg roll wrapper. Sold dried in disks, rice paper is brittle and fragile when dry, yet supple and elastic once softened in water. Summer rolls use the rice paper in its softened state, while egg rolls go a step further with a little deep-frying action.

¾ oz bundle of dried rice vermicelli noodles, soaked in just-boiled water for 8 minutes and then drained, rinsed, and cut into 3-inch pieces

1 small head of Little Gem lettuce, shredded

1 carrot, peeled and julienned

3½ oz picked white crab meat or leftover cooked shredded pork, chicken, or duck (optional)

small handful of fresh cilantro, finely chopped

10 to 15 egg roll wrappers (skins)

10 large cooked peeled shrimp, sliced in half lengthwise

a few sprigs of mint, leaves picked

bundle of chives

For the dipping sauce:

2 tablespoons hoi sin sauce

1 tablespoon Homemade Sriracha (*see page 109, or use ready-made*) or chili oil

1 teaspoon smooth peanut butter

1 tablespoon rice vinegar

½ tablespoon water

Fold the bottom flap over the filling, tucking it under the filling a little.

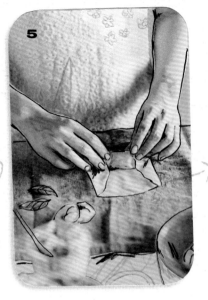

Then fold the 2 sides in tightly.

Add a couple of mint leaves and line up 3 shrimp halves horizontally in a row on the empty wrapper above the filling,

Place, seam-side down, under a damp dish towel, while you prepare the rest.

Serve the rolls with the dipping sauce, or alternatively with Nuoc Cham (*see page 34*).

Fold the whole thing over again. The moistened wrapper should still be tacky enough to stick to itself.

Place a couple of chives so that they sit in line horizontally with the pouch of filling but poke out of the side.

These differ from summer rolls slightly, besides the obvious method of cooking. The fresh herbs are replaced with garlic and shallots, the salad greens with cooking vegetables, and the salad is served on the side for you to wrap your egg roll up in and dip in the sauce, almost like an inside-out roll. I prefer these with glass noodles rather than rice vermicelli, since they withstand the deep-frying better.

VIETNAMESE EGG ROLLS

Mix the ground pork with the wood ear mushrooms, garlic, and shallots. Add the sugar and stir to combine.

Heat a wok with 1 tablespoon of the cooking oil and fry the pork mixture until it is no longer raw. Remove and let cool. Combine with the noodles and carrot in a bowl.

Meanwhile, prepare a bowl of hand-hot water. Lay out a clean, dry dish towel in front of you. Immerse an egg roll wrapper in the water for a few seconds—it should start softening up. Remove from the water and lay out flat on the dish towel. Add about 2 tablespoons of the filling to the center of the wrapper but slightly nearer the bottom closest to you. Fold the bottom flap over the filling, tucking it under the filling a little, then fold the 2 sides in tightly and fold the whole thing over again. The moistened wrapper should still be tacky enough to stick to itself. Place on a plate, seam-side down, under a damp dish towel while you prepare the rest.

Preheat the oven to 225°F. Wipe out the inside of the wok with paper towels and add the remaining cooking oil. Heat to 350°F, or until bubbles appear up the sides of a wooden chopstick when inserted into the hot oil. Fry the egg rolls, in batches, for 6 or so minutes, turning once if the oil doesn't cover them, until the wrapper has bubbled and the rolls are golden brown. Remove with a slotted spoon and let drain on a wire rack placed on a baking pan in the oven while you fry the rest.

Serve with nuoc cham and whole lettuce leaves with mint and Thai basil leaves for people to help themselves.

3½ oz ground pork

1 dried wood ear mushroom, soaked in just-boiled water for 30 minutes and then drained, rolled up, and shredded

3 garlic cloves, minced

3 shallots, finely sliced

1 teaspoon sugar

1 cup cooking oil, divided

3½ oz dried glass noodles (*see page 49*), soaked in just-boiled water for 5 minutes, drained, then rinsed and cut into 3-inch pieces

1 carrot, peeled and julienned

10 to 15 egg roll wrappers

To serve
Nuoc Cham (*see page 34*)

whole lettuce leaves

mint leaves

Thai basil leaves

This is one of my favorite Vietnamese noodle dishes. When I'm after something a little more substantial, I use Jiangxi noodles, the thicker version of the "bun" type, and almost spaghetti-like in thickness. When I want a lighter meal, I'll choose vermicelli. Crisp, crunchy vegetables give the impression of a healthy meal, even if I do then go and top it with something deep-fried, but you can also use grilled pork, or lemon grass-marinated chicken instead. Usually served at room temperature, they also make a great packed lunch. Just go easy on the garlic in the nuoc cham if you're using it, unless you have very forgiving colleagues.

VIETNAMESE EGG ROLL NOODLES

SERVES 1

3½ oz dried rice vermicelli or Jiangxi noodles (*see page 48*), the former soaked in just-boiled water for 10 minutes and drained, the latter soaked for 30 minutes and drained

½ small cucumber, peeled and thinly sliced into half-moons

1 small carrot, peeled and shredded

1 Little Gem or iceberg lettuce leaf, finely sliced

a few sprigs of fresh cilantro, coarsely chopped

1 sprig of mint, leaves picked and thinly sliced

1 quantity Nuoc Cham (*see page 34*)

2 Vietnamese Egg Rolls (*see opposite*)

Place the noodles in a bundle in the middle of your bowl, and line one edge with the half-moons of cucumber. Arrange little piles of carrot and lettuce on top of the noodles, and scatter with the herbs.

Drizzle the nuoc cham evenly over the dish, and set the egg rolls on top. To eat, stir and toss everything together with chopsticks to amalgamate.

INSTANT NOODLE PIMPS

Like any good Asian kid, I love instant noodles. I grew up on them. I'm not talking about the cheap kind you buy in supermarkets; these are way better. Sometimes in life, you may not have the time or inclination to cook a big meal. Whatever the reason, enjoy those instant noodles. There are hundreds of varieties. Experiment with them and embellish them. Here's a little help with that.

NOODLES

There are so many brands of instant noodle that it could take a lifetime to try them all. There are the standard ramen blocks with soup sachets, then there are types that are to be served dressed rather than in soup, and there are those that come in their own cup. Experiment with them, play around, and figure out your favorite.

STOCK

First things first. You can throw that flavoring sachet away and make these with chicken stock, or add soy sauce, sesame oil, or fish sauce to water. But let's face it, the sachets are easy. They're tasty. Instant noodles come in so many flavors now that you can, for example, match a seafood one to one you'll pimp with shrimp, for example.

MEAT & SHELLFISH

You can go for just about anything. Leftover roasted meats, raw meat sliced thinly and swooshed in the stock to cook, uncooked shrimp, fish fillets, smoked pork sausages, frankfurters, SPAM—they all work. You can even use canned sardines in tomato sauce, warmed though with a little chili oil, to dress the noodles instead of having them in soup.

EGGS

Top your noodles with a fried egg, or a soft-cooked egg, or crack an egg into the broth to poach while the noodles are cooking, too. Place an egg in a metal container with a lid (like a small saucepan) with just-boiled water for 10 minutes for an onsen tamago (hot spring egg), where the egg white is slightly floppy and the yolk firmer.

HERBS & AROMATICS

Cilantro and scallion are king. Slivered fresh kaffir lime leaves added to the broth are also delicious. A squeeze of fresh lime juice goes a long way, and you can also buy tubs of fried shallots to scatter on top. Basil, Vietnamese hot mint (rau ram), perilla leaves, and dill also work well when used with appropriate flavors—beef stock with basil and hot mint, for instance, like a faux pho.

VEGETABLES

Pretty essential these. Bok choy, choy sum, gai laan, sugar snap peas, snow peas, green snap beans, Belgian endive, green sprouting broccoli, chard, spinach, watercress, baby corn, quartered tomatoes, bean sprouts, and iceberg or romaine lettuce all work marvelously and will cook happily in the broth with the noodles.

GARNISHES

You may have noticed that I like chiles—a lot. So, I almost always have some form of chile going, and noodles are no exception. Sliced chiles, chili oil, Tabasco sauce, sriracha (*see page 109 for homemade, or use ready-made*), Chile & Ginger Sauce (*see page 64*), chopped chiles in a little rice vinegar, Nuoc Cham (*see page 34*), and nam prik pao (a Thai roasted chie paste) are all winners.

This is the ultimate instant noodle pimp. It's filthy. It was developed after the Korean War when the Koreans used store cupboard ingredients left behind on U.S. military bases. Canned meats and processed cheese are the main ingredients for this stew; embrace it in its guilty glory, especially if you're hung over or attempting to survive the apocalypse and you happen to have a working gas stove.

BUDDAE JJIGAE

SERVES 2

1 tablespoon sesame oil

1 teaspoon minced garlic

2 tablespoons gochujang (*see page 16*)

1¾ oz cabbage kimchi (*see page 143 for homemade*), coarsely chopped

3 scallions, white parts sliced into 1¼-inch lengths, green parts thinly sliced diagonally

2 wieners (preferably the type bottled in brine), sliced diagonally into thick slices

6 oz canned SPAM, cut into thick slices

1 cup canned baked beans

3¼ cups water

3 oz package instant ramen noodles (*see page 49*)

2 processed cheese slices

Heat a saucepan or clay pot (*see page 11*) on low heat and add the sesame oil. Then add the garlic and fry for 30 seconds until fragrant.

Add the gochujang and mix well. Add the kimchi, the whites of the scallions, the wieners, SPAM, and the baked beans, and then the water. Try to keep each component in a different part of the pan so that it's like a layered casserole. Next, submerge the instant ramen block in the liquid. Cover and let simmer for 4 minutes.

Remove the lid and wiggle the tines of a fork in the noodles to loosen them. If it's looking a little dry, add a touch more water. Finally, set the cheese slices on top, cover, and let stand for a minute to allow the cheese to melt. Scatter with the scallion greens, to serve.

CHAPTER

3

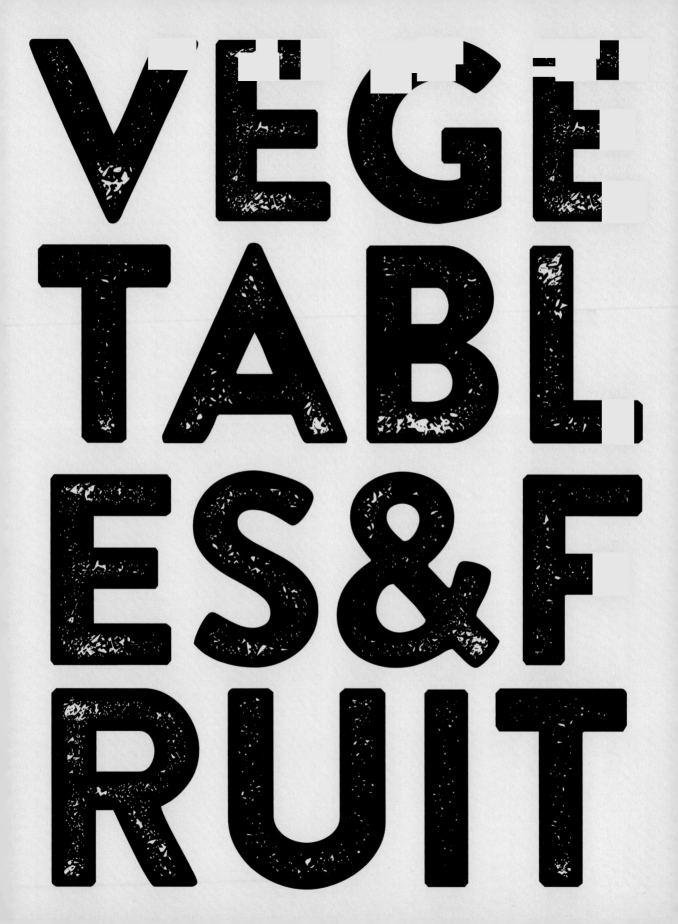

VEGETABLES & FRUIT

The fruit and vegetable section of the Asian supermarket is often bewildering, mainly because the green leafy vegetables can look very similar, and are usually labeled with their Chinese, Thai, or Vietnamese name, depending on the specialism of the supermarket you are in. Some don't even have English names. If in doubt, as a general rule, I wash them well and stir-fry them with garlic until I've worked out what they are. Hopefully, the images here will help you recognize them.

HERBS & AROMATICS

Lemon grass, galangal, and kaffir lime leaves are the holy trinity of Thai cooking. Cilantro, mint, Thai basil, Vietnamese coriander, pandan leaves, and betel leaves are also worth exploring.

SHISO LEAVES

Shiso leaves are commonly used in Korean and Japanese cuisine. Also called perilla, they have a medicinal fragrance, and are a little minty, with a hint of aniseed.

VEGETABLES

ALLIUMS

Chinese chives, flowering chives, garlic scapes, and scallions all belong to this same family, Allium, but range from being very much like onion in flavor to being closer to garlic. The stems of each have a different shape that suits different uses. Chinese chives (also called garlic chives) are flat, for example, and are often used to flavor dumplings and breads while garlic scapes have round cylindrical stems and are more often used as a vegetable in their own right, as are flowering chives.

(1,2 & 3) MELONS & GOURDS

Even though winter melon (1) and bitter melon (2) are both called melons, they couldn't be further from each other flavorwise. One is soft and inoffensive, the other bitter and aggressive. The loofah gourd (3), however, is wonderfully spongy, as you might imagine from its name.

(4) DAIKON
(ASIAN RADISH)

You can pickle it, eat it raw, braise it, and even make it into a cake. This is truly the most versatile of the vegetables.

(5) LOTUS ROOTS

Lotus roots are visually stunning, with their arrangement of holes through the root. They don't taste like much, but provide a texture. They must always be cooked, because they are not safe to eat raw.

FRESH MUSHROOMS

Enoki, shimeji, and king oyster mushrooms are the main varieties available. While enoki and shimeji are delicate and require only a little cooking, the king oyster is meaty and robust.

LEAFY GREENS

(6) CHINESE CABBAGE
(CHINESE LEAF OR NAPA CABBAGE)

Large and pale green or yellow in color, this is eaten raw or cooked, and is often used to make kimchi, too.

(7) CHINESE BROCCOLI
(KAI LAAN)

Dark green with a long thick stem and a small broccoli-like head on top, sometimes with small yellow flowers, Chinese broccoli is iron-rich in flavor and often steamed or stir-fried.

(8) BOK CHOY

This comes in green and white varieties, and large and baby forms, and is often steamed or stir-fried.

(9) CHOY SUM

Like bok choy, but longer-stemmed and thinner, choy sum is stir-fried, steamed, or served in noodle soups.

(10) WATER SPINACH
(TUNG CHOY OR KANG KONG)

These long, arrow-shaped leaves with long stems that are round and hollow are usually stir-fried with pungent flavorings.

(11) PEA SHOOTS
(DOU MIU)

With short, squat, rounded leaves, pea shoots are usually stir-fried but sometimes served in soups.

6.

7.

8.

9.

10.

11.

12.

13.

14.

15.

(12) MUSTARD GREENS (KAI CHOY)

These are what you would find pickled (*see page 162*). They have a bit of a spicy bite to them. You can pickle them yourself, braise them, or add them to soups.

(13) CHRYSANTHEMUM GREENS (TONG HO)

These flat, rounded leaves are slightly bitter and medicinal in flavor, and are often used in hot pots and soups.

(14) RED / GREEN AMARANTH

The red amaranth leaves are easily distinguishable, since they have a red tinge on the underside of the leaf. Sturdy and iron-rich, the green version is often used in soups, though the red is reserved for stir-frying, because the color inside them releases a vibrant pink juice.

(15) MIZUNA

Used mostly in Japanese cooking, mizuna leaves are delicate and long, and spiked at the edges. They taste a bit like arugula.

HOW I LIKE TO EAT LEAFY GREENS

In Soup (noodle soup, broths, stews): Chinese cabbage, pea shoots, chrysanthemum greens, bok choy, choy sum, mustard greens, green amaranth, mizuna

Stir-fried with ginger: Chinese broccoli (boil in water with 1 teaspoon sugar for 2 minutes, drain, and then stir-fry)

Stir-fried with garlic: Pea shoots, bok choy, Chinese cabbage, red / green amaranth

Stir-fried with garlic & fermented bean curd: Water spinach, Chinese broccoli (boil in water with 1 teaspoon sugar for 2 minutes, drain, and then stir-fry)

Steamed & drizzled with oyster sauce: Bok choy, choy sum, Chinese broccoli

Raw: Chinese cabbage, mizuna

FRUIT

(16) MANGOSTEEN

Often called the "queen of fruits," mangosteens are little purple spheres and are one of my favorite fruits. Squeeze the rind until the fruit splits, then pull apart to reveal the soft white flesh inside. The larger globes may have a seed in them, which you can spit out. Soft, creamy, and fragrant, these don't come cheap when imported, but are incredibly delicious.

(17) RAMBUTAN

These are distinctive from their red, hairy outer shells. Crack the skin open and pop the fruit in your mouth, but there is a seed in the center you will need to spit out.

(18) LONGANS

Called "dragon's eye" in Cantonese, these are similar in size to lychees, but are beige and smooth-skinned. Wash them, pop the skin open with your teeth, then peel the skin away to reveal the flesh.

(19) LYCHEES

Pink-skinned and a little knobbly, lychees must be peeled and pitted before eating. Purée the fruit and reduce to a syrup to flavor drinks, or ice the lychee flesh and eat with ice cream.

(20) ASIAN PEARS

These are yellow and round; the skin is thin and the flesh has an almost icy texture to it. Not a great deal of flavor other than sweetness, but one of my trusted hangover alleviators.

(21) DRAGONFRUIT

It's a dramatic-looking fruit, with pink skin and black-seeded, snow-white flesh. The skin should not be eaten. To prepare, slice the fruit in half and scoop the white flesh out with a large spoon.

(22) PAPAYA

Long and oval in shape, ripe papayas are orange-fleshed. They're my least favorite fruit; they're a bit too reminiscent of rotting fruit. I can just about bear them with a squeeze of lime. To make classic Thai salads, go for unripe and green fruits.

(23) MANGO

Mangoes are widely available and you can buy them in most general supermarkets. Alphonso mangos, available only for a short season, are some of the best, and are honeylike in flavor and creamy. Many Indian and Caribbean grocers sell mango purée in cans.

(24) DURIAN

Often called the "king of fruits," durian is infamous for its revolting odor. Banned in many hotels and on public transportation in Asia, durian is pretty good once you get past the stink. The fruit itself is encased in a hard, spiked shell; once you get it open, bright yellow lobes of creamy flesh can be eaten, made into ice cream, cakes, and candies. You will often find the lobes frozen or in the chilled-foods section of the supermarket.

Tom yum is a classic Thai soup. It has a light, bright, and spicy broth made by simmering aromatic herbs and chiles. The key components—lemon grass, galangal, and kaffir lime leaves—are completely essential to the flavor of this. Don't be tempted to replace the water with chicken stock; it's not supposed to taste like chicken. Its fragrance should come from the citrus. Using coconut water was a trick I picked up from my travels in Thailand. It adds depth and sweetness without being overpowering. The brilliant thing is that all the flavorings can be kept in the freezer, so tom yum is on hand as long as you have a couple of vegetables and a lime.

SERVES

2

AS AN APPETIZER
OR LIGHT MEAL

TOM YUM GOONG

1¾ cups water

1 cup coconut water (NOT coconut milk)—you can buy coconut water in cartons; go for the unflavored, 100% natural variety (optional)

2 red bird's-eye chiles (more if you're a chile fiend), snapped in half

3 slices of fresh galangal, peeled

5 kaffir lime leaves, divided

2 lemon grass stalks, woody outer layers removed

6 cherry tomatoes

handful of fresh oyster mushrooms, washed and coarsely torn

6 raw jumbo shrimp in their shells, defrosted in cold water if frozen

1 teaspoon nam prik pao (Thai roasted chile paste)

1 lime, halved, for juicing

2 tablespoons fish sauce, divided

a few sprigs of fresh cilantro, coarsely chopped

Simmer the water and coconut water in a saucepan with the chiles, galangal, 2 of the lime leaves, and the lemon grass for 20 minutes, covered. Strain the stock through a sieve into a fresh saucepan and discard the flavoring ingredients.

Add the cherry tomatoes and mushrooms and simmer over medium heat for 3 minutes, and then add the shrimp and the remaining lime leaves, torn in half. Bring to a simmer, then remove the pan from the heat. Let stand for 5 minutes, then stir in the nam prik pao.

To each bowl, add the juice of half a lime and 1 tablespoon of the fish sauce. Pour the soup into the bowls and toss the cilantro on top. It's a spicy soup, so reduce the number of chiles if you can't take the heat.

⇥OTHER IDEAS
Replace 1¼ cups of the water with coconut milk to make the richer Tom Kha Goong.

Lemon grass has a special kind of flavor. You can't really substitute its floral, citrus flavor with anything else. Deliciously perfumed, it goes very well with seafood, and these mussels are creamy and rich, filling but delicate. Lemon grass keeps very well in the freezer.

MUSSELS IN LEMON-GRASS BROTH

SERVES
2 or **1**
AS AN APPETIZER / AS A MAIN

Check over the mussels, throwing out any with damaged shells or any open ones that won't shut after tapping them lightly on a hard surface. Pull away the stringy beards and scrape off any barnacles with a knife, then rinse well.

Heat the cooking oil with the garlic in a saucepan on medium heat until fragrant but not browned. Add the coconut milk and water and bring to a boil. Add the woody outer layers of the lemon grass stalks, cover, and simmer for 10 minutes on medium-low heat.

Meanwhile, pound the minced lemon grass inner parts in a mortar and pestle to release their fragrance. Add the sugar, grated lime zest, and fish sauce, mixing well. Fish the lemon grass outer layers out of the coconut-milk mixture and discard, and then add the chiles and lime leaves.

Add the mussels to the coconut-milk mixture, turn the heat up to medium, and cover. Cook for 3 to 5 minutes, stirring once—they are ready when all the shells have opened up (discard any that have failed to open). Remove from the heat and add the sugar, lemon grass, and fish sauce mixture along with the shallot, and then put the lid back on for another minute.

Dish out into 2 deep bowls, scatter with the cilantro and squeeze over the lime juice before serving. For a more substantial meal, you can place some precooked rice vermicelli in the bottom of each bowl before adding the mussels in lemon grass broth.

14 oz live mussels

1 tablespoon cooking oil

2 garlic cloves, minced

7 fl oz can coconut milk

½ cup water

2 lemon grass stalks, woody outer layers removed but reserved, tender inner parts minced

1 teaspoon superfine sugar

grated zest and juice of ½ lime

1½ tablespoons fish sauce

2 red bird's-eye chiles, broken in half

3 kaffir lime leaves

1 red Asian shallot or banana shallot, finely sliced

handful of fresh cilantro, coarsely chopped

Cabbage. Cabbage. Not exactly a sexy word, is it? To most, cabbage evokes memories of a flatulent, overcooked pile of sludge. However, this dish is anything but. Bright green leaves stir-fried until just tender are perked up with this tangy sauce.

CABBAGE IN VINEGAR SAUCE

SERVES 4 WITH OTHER DISHES

Mix all the sauce ingredients together and set aside.

Bring a saucepan of water to a boil and blanch the Chinese cabbage in it for 1 minute, then drain well.

While the cabbage is still hot, heat the oil in a wok on medium heat and fry the Sichuan peppercorns until the oil is fragrant, and then remove them with a slotted spoon. Add the dried chiles and fry until they are brown but not burned. Add the ginger, garlic, and scallion whites, and stir-fry briefly. Add the blanched cabbage and stir-fry on high heat until heated through. (You want to do this part at high heat to get some smoky flavor into the vegetables.) Add the sauce and stir-fry until the sauce has thickened.

Place the vegetables on a plate and garnish with the scallion greens.

1 lb 5 oz Chinese cabbage (Chinese leaf or Napa cabbage)

2 to 3 tablespoons cooking oil

2 teaspoons Sichuan peppercorns

a few dried chiles, seeded and cut into small pieces

small piece of fresh ginger root, peeled and minced

3 garlic cloves, minced

1 heaped tablespoon chopped scallion, white parts only, green parts reserved and finely sliced

For the sauce:

2½ tablespoons Chinkiang black vinegar or other good-quality Chinese vinegar

1 tablespoon sugar

½ teaspoon salt

2 teaspoons light soy sauce

1 rounded teaspoon cornstarch

1 tablespoon cold water

Garlic scapes are the sturdiest of the allium family that you can find in Chinatown. The stems are round and thick, smelling pungently of garlic that mellows out in cooking, and can take a fair bit of heat. If you can't find them, use scallions or Chinese chives instead (*see page 82*), and reduce the cooking time.

SERVES

2

AS A SIDE DISH

GARLIC SCAPES STIR-FRIED *with* SHRIMP & EGG

Mix the soy sauce with the cornstarch in a bowl, stir in the shrimp, and let marinate while you prepare the rest of the dish.

Beat the eggs in another bowl with the black pepper, white pepper, salt, and rice wine. Cut the garlic scapes into pieces 1½ inches long.

Place a wok on medium heat and swirl 1 tablespoon of the cooking oil around inside it. When the oil is shimmering, add the garlic scapes and stir-fry for a good 5 minutes so that they take on some color and soften. Turn the heat up to maximum and add the shrimp, stir-frying them with the scapes for 30 seconds so that they turn a little pink. Push to one side and add the remaining tablespoon of cooking oil.

Pour in the eggs and let them set for 10 seconds. Then, using a spatula, scramble them into the shrimp and scapes. Remove from the heat so that the eggs remain soft and creamy, and then serve with some rice or noodles.

1 teaspoon light soy sauce

1 teaspoon cornstarch

7 oz peeled raw jumbo shrimp

4 free-range eggs

pinch of ground black pepper

pinch of ground white pepper

pinch of salt

1 tablespoon Shaoxing rice wine

4 stalks of garlic scapes

2 tablespoons cooking oil, divided

splash of sesame oil

➺ OTHER IDEAS

Stir-fry the garlic scapes with thinly sliced marinated meat, tofu (bean curd), or mushrooms, make pesto with them, or shred them raw and add to the dressing for the Smacked Cucumber Salad (see page 33).

There is just a hint of seasoning here, since the garlic scapes and the bacon are so aromatic on their own. The garlic scapes are like a grassy, sweeter garlic and are robust when raw; mellow when cooked. I especially enjoy the flavor of them when they are a little charred. Like a lot of dishes in Asian cuisines, just a small amount of meat is needed to impart flavor rather than to dominate. I often eat this simply with a bowl of rice.

SERVES
4
AS A SIDE
DISH

THAI-STYLE GARLIC SCAPES STIR-FRIED *with* BACON

14 oz garlic scapes (*see page 82*)
6 strips of smoked bacon
1 tablespoon cooking oil
1 tablespoon fish sauce
1 teaspoon sugar
½ teaspoon ground white pepper

Wash the garlic scapes thoroughly, pat dry with paper towels, and then chop into pieces 2 inches long. Slice the bacon into slivers.

Heat the oil in a wok on high heat until almost smoking. Add the bacon and stir-fry until some of the fat has rendered and the bacon is starting to get crisp.

Turn the heat up to maximum and add the garlic scapes. Stir-fry briskly for 3 minutes, and then add the fish sauce, sugar, and white pepper. Stir-fry for another minute, and then remove from the heat. Spoon out onto a plate to serve.

These are called "bing" and are sold all over China in various forms from the street. A popular version is made with egg instead of a pancake—the egg is poured all over a hot plate and spread out until wafer thin, then topped with scallions and other flavorings, before it's folded into itself to make a parcel. I prefer these breads (often called pancakes), since they are able to soak up that delicious sauce far more easily. You will often see these made with scallions, but Chinese chives are brilliant here too, because they are mellower and sweeter.

CHINESE CHIVE BREADS

SERVES 4 TO 6 AS A SNACK

1¼ cups all-purpose flour, plus extra for dusting
½ teaspoon salt
⅓ cup just-boiled water
large bunch of Chinese chives or scallions
3 tablespoons toasted sesame oil
2 tablespoons cooking oil, divided

For the dipping sauce:
1 tablespoon chili oil with sediment (*see page 12*)
2 tablespoons light soy sauce
2 tablespoons Chinkiang black vinegar
1 teaspoon sugar
a few slivers of julienned fresh ginger root

Add the flour and salt to a large mixing bowl. Pour the just-boiled water into the flour, little by little, mixing it in with a wooden spoon. Let cool for 10 minutes. Transfer to a floured work surface and knead the dough for 3 minutes, or until it is smooth and silky. Place back in the bowl, cover with a clean dish towel, and let stand for 30 minutes.

Meanwhile, slice the chives or scallions very finely. Mix all the ingredients for the dipping sauce together in an appropriate bowl.

At this point, preheat your oven to low to keep the breads warm, because they will need to be cooked in batches of 1 to 2 at a time.

Separate the dough into 4 pieces. Dust the work surface with flour.

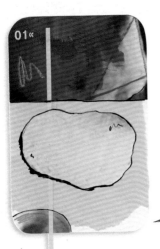

Roll 1 piece of dough out into a large circle about ⅛ inch thick.

Brush one side with a little of the sesame oil

Roll it up into a cigar shape, starting from the bottom upward.

Coil the dough around tightly into a snail shape

Flatten the coil, then roll it out into a large circle.

Brush it again with sesame oil and scatter with one-quarter of the chives or scallions.

Repeat the cigar rolling and the snail coiling and then carefully roll out again.

The chives (or scallions) will burst out of the dough a little, but this isn't a bad thing.

9 Repeat with the other 3 pieces of dough, separating them with nonstick parchment paper so that they don't stick together.

Heat 1 tablespoon of the cooking oil in a nonstick or cast-iron skillet on medium heat. Fry a pancake on one side, pressing down any layers that have puffed up using a spatula, until golden and crisp. Turn over and repeat. Add the second tablespoon of cooking oil to the skillet after you've fried the second pancake.

Slice each pancake into quarters and serve with the dipping sauce.

- **9 oz** fresh winter melon
- **1 tablespoon** dried shrimps
- **2 tablespoons** cooking oil
- **1** scallion, diagonally sliced, white and green parts separated
- **1 tablespoon** peeled and chopped fresh ginger root
- **large pinch** of salt
- **3 tablespoons** water
- **pinch** of ground white pepper

WINTER MELON BRAISED *with* DRIED SHRIMPS

SERVES 4

Winter melon, used most often in soups, tastes of very little, so one might ask why we don't just feed it to the pigs? Than answer is, it has a wonderfully light, nonfibrous texture that has a way of soaking up all the flavors around it.

Peel the winter melon using a vegetable peeler, then cut into thick matchsticks.

Wash the dried shrimps and then soak in a bowl of hot water for 2 minutes. Drain and set aside.

Set a wok on high heat and add the cooking oil, swirling it to coat the sides. When hot, add the whites of the scallion and the ginger and stir-fry over high heat for about 20 seconds, or until fragrant. Add the soaked shrimps and winter melon sticks and stir-fry for 2 minutes.

Add the salt, water, and white pepper and stir-fry until the water has evaporated. Remove from the heat and taste to check the seasoning. Serve in deep bowls garnished with the sliced scallion greens.

Bitter melon is something of an acquired taste. Chances are you might hate it. But you might love it, especially if you drink Guinness or pale ale. It's kind of a unique vegetable in that respect; we usually prize sweetness in vegetables and fruit, but this is the exact opposite. Look for bright, light green melons, since these tend to be less aggressively bitter. The Indian equivalent, called kerala, is darker green and knobbly and is much more bitter in flavor. It is believed that bitter melon has a blood glucose-lowering effect, though this is probably negated by how much sugar I like to use in the sauce.

BITTER MELON STUFFED
with PORK & SHRIMP

SERVES 2

1 bitter melon

3 tablespoons salt

2¾ oz ground pork

2¾ oz raw peeled shrimp, minced

1 scallion, finely sliced

1 teaspoon peeled and grated fresh ginger root

½ dried wood ear mushroom, soaked in just-boiled water for 30 minutes and then drained, then curled into a cigar shape and thinly sliced

1 teaspoon cornstarch

½ tablespoon light soy sauce

1 teaspoon sesame oil

1 tablespoon cooking oil

For the sauce:

1¼ cups water

1 tablespoon sugar

2 tablespoons oyster sauce

1 tablespoon light soy sauce

1 teaspoon cornstarch, mixed with 1 tablespoon cold water

Slice the bitter melon into disks about 1½ inches wide. Use a teaspoon to scrape the inner membrane and seeds out. Boil a little water and, in a large bowl, dissolve the salt in the water. Add enough cold water to cover the bitter melon disks and let soak for 30 minutes (this reduces the bitterness).

Meanwhile, in a separate bowl, mix the pork, shrimp, scallion, ginger, mushroom, cornstarch, soy sauce, and sesame oil well with your hands. Cover with plastic wrap and let marinate while the bitter melon is soaking.

Drain the bitter melon and pat dry with paper towels, and then stuff with the pork and shrimp mixture. Add the cooking oil to a wok and set on medium heat for 1 minute. Fry the bitter melon disks for 4 minutes, or until golden brown, then flip them over and fry them on the other side for 4 minutes.

For the sauce, combine the water, sugar, oyster sauce, and soy sauce and add to the wok. Cover and cook on medium heat for 10 minutes. Add the cornstarch solution to the wok to thicken the sauce; this shouldn't take more than a couple of minutes. Transfer the bitter melon to a dish, drizzle the sauce on top, and serve with steamed rice.

➥ OTHER IDEAS
Stir-fry bitter melon with pork and soy sauce, cook it in black bean sauce, or, if you're a real sadist, juice it.

2 disks, 1¼in wide, cut from
a large, peeled daikon (Asian radish),
plus an additional slice for garnish

2 dried shiitake mushrooms, soaked
in just-boiled water for 30 minutes
and then drained

2½ cups dashi
(*see page 209 for homemade*)

1 tablespoon mirin

1 tablespoon light soy sauce

1 scallion, green part only,
julienned

JAPANESE SIMMERED DAIKON

SERVES
2

This dish celebrates the purest flavor of the daikon (Asian radish). I eat this dish a lot when I'm craving lighter meals—enjoyed with a little rice and some stir-fried vegetables, you'll feel positively saintly. For a fuller meal, you can add chicken drumsticks to simmer in the broth first.

Cut a cross into each daikon disk about half their width deep. Remove the stems from the shiitake mushrooms and add to the dashi in a saucepan, then add the daikon, cut-side down, with the mirin and soy sauce. Bring the dashi to a boil over high heat, then reduce the heat and simmer gently for 20 minutes partially covered. Turn the daikon slices over and simmer for another 20 minutes.

To serve, add a slice of daikon to a bowl and fish out a mushroom. Place the mushroom, cap-side up, in the bowl. Grate the additional daikon slice on the finest grater, then mix 1 teaspoon of it with half the julienned scallion greens and pile into a mushroom cap. If your mushroom is a little on the small side, it won't hurt if it overflows. Repeat with the rest of the grated daikon and scallion greens and the remaining mushroom. Spoon the dashi stock around the daikon disks.

➤➤OTHER IDEAS
You can flavor this further by placing marinated slices of fish on top of the daikon disks before steaming them briefly with the lid on.

The incredibly versatile daikon (Asian radish) is used in many countries, often finely grated to accompany sushi, stewed in meaty broths, and even curried. Long, white, and slender and, when raw, it is crisp with a mild pepperiness that is excellent julienned in slaws. Its sturdy structure means it can also be slow-cooked in stews without breaking down, and one of the most famous uses for it is in this turnip "cake"—a steamed dish that, once cooled, is then fried until crispy on both sides. It's classic Cantonese, eaten often at dim sum and celebrations, such as Chinese New Year. The carrot is my addition; I like it for its sweetness and color.

TURNIP CAKE (LOH BAK GOH)

1 lb 2 oz daikon (Asian radish), peeled

2 carrots, peeled

1½ teaspoons salt

1½ tablespoons superfine sugar

1 scant teaspoon ground white pepper

¼ cup cooking oil, divided, plus extra for oiling

5 shallots, thinly sliced

3 garlic cloves, minced

2 Chinese sausages, diced

4 dried shiitake mushrooms, soaked in just-boiled water for 30 minutes, then drained, stems discarded, and diced

1 tablespoon dried shrimps, washed and then soaked in just-boiled water for 15 minutes, then drained, squeezed dry, and coarsely chopped

3 tablespoons Shaoxing rice wine

1¼ cups rice flour (not glutinous)

3 tablespoons potato starch

6 scallions, finely sliced

To serve

soy sauce

chili oil

Coarsely grate one-third of the daikon into a saucepan, before grating the rest in finely. This is to give the cake a little texture. Then grate the carrots finely into the saucepan. Add 1 cup of water, along with the salt, sugar, and white pepper. Simmer for 5 to 10 minutes on medium heat, or until the vegetable matter is soft and the pan is very dry.

Heat 1 tablespoon of the cooking oil in another saucepan over medium heat and fry the shallots and garlic for 30 seconds, ensuring that they don't color. Add the Chinese sausage and cook for 5 minutes, or until all the fat in the sausage has been released. Add the shiitake mushrooms and the dried shrimps, then add the rice wine and cover immediately. Let it steam like this for a couple of minutes, and then uncover and cook, stirring, until the wine has evaporated. Remove from the heat.

Oil a loaf pan or a shallow cake pan and set aside. Beat the rice flour and potato starch with 2 cups water in a large mixing bowl. Add the scallions, meat mixture, and the cooked daikon and carrot and mix well. Add another 2 tablespoons of the cooking oil. Pour into the oiled pan and steam for 1 hour in a metal steamer. Or set the oiled pan into a larger baking pan half filled with boiling water. Cover in foil and bake in an oven preheated to 300°F for 1 hour. The cake will still have a wobbly center. Let cool completely and then let chill for a couple of hours.

To serve, heat the remaining tablespoon of cooking oil in a nonstick skillet on medium heat. Run a knife around the edge of the cake and invert onto a plate. Cut slices as thick as your forefinger and fry on medium heat for a few minutes on each side to form a golden-brown crust. Serve with soy sauce and chili oil.

1 loofah gourd, ridges cut off and peeled
1 tablespoon cooking oil
2 garlic cloves, minced
1 bird's-eye chile, coarsely chopped
handful of fresh oyster or shiitake mushrooms
1 tablespoon light soy sauce
1 tablespoon oyster sauce
½ teaspoon sugar
3 tablespoons water
4 kaffir lime leaves, tough stems removed,
rolled and very thinly sliced

LOOFAH GOURD STIR-FRIED *with* KAFFIR LIME LEAVES

SERVES

2

AS A SIDE
DISH

Loofah gourds are also called luffa, or angled or ridged gourds, thanks to their appearance. They are long and dark green, fatter at one end, and narrow down into a point at the other. The skin is best peeled off—cut down the ridges with a knife before peeling with a vegetable peeler—because it can be very tough and bitter. The gourd is eaten when green and young; it's only when it becomes aged and fibrous that you should consider using it as a body scrubber (don't actually—they're processed first!). Keep the spongy innards and the seeds, since these are edible and make up the body of them. They taste mildly of cucumber, a little sweet, and soak up flavors beautifully when you stir-fry them or cook them in soups. This recipe uses the fragrance of kaffir lime leaves to give a normal vegetable side a new dimension.

"Roll cut" your loofah gourd: hold it in front of you and make the first cut at a 45° angle. Roll the loofah 90° away from you and cut again, repeating until you get to the end—this is so that it has the maximum surface area.

Heat the cooking oil in a wok on high heat to just below smoking, then reduce the heat to medium. Add the garlic and chile and stir-fry briskly for 30 seconds. Turn the heat up high and add the loofah gourd and mushrooms, stir-frying as you go.

Add the soy sauce, oyster sauce, and sugar and stir so that everything is well coated. Add the water, cover the wok, and steam for 2 minutes, or until the loofah becomes tender. Remove the lid, throw in the lime leaves, and stir-fry for another minute, or until the mixture is fairly dry but glossy and not sticking to the pan. Spoon out into a serving dish.

➤ OTHER IDEAS
Stir-fry the gourd with scrambled eggs, curry it with tomatoes and Indian spices, or pair it with tofu puffs and egg gravy (*see Seafood Ho Fun in Egg Gravy, page 63*).

Lotus root must always be cooked because it's not safe to eat raw. Now, I know that deep-frying isn't something you should do all the time, but I tried these baked and they're ... different. Tougher. Much like when you buy "healthy" potato chips in the hope that they will taste just as good as the regular ones and all they are is an overly crunchy disappointment. So plow on with the deep-frying and eat a carrot stick to assuage the guilt. (That's how it works, right?) You can try a variety of seasonings, as long as they are dry. A anything wet will make these chips soggy, but any mixture should have some salt in it for essential seasoning.

SERVES
6
AS A SNACK

LOTUS ROOT CHIPS

1 teaspoon distilled vinegar
1 lotus root
1¼ cups vegetable oil, for deep-frying

For the seasoning:
3 parts fine table salt
1 part dried chile flakes
2 parts nori (*see page 188*), toasted under the broiler until crisp, and crumbled into flakes
2 parts white sesame seeds, toasted, mixed with **1 part** sugar

Add the vinegar to a large bowl of water. Using a mandoline, slice the lotus root 1/16 inch thick and carefully place in the water to soak for 10 minutes. (The vinegar prevents discoloration.)

Grind the seasoning ingredients together using a mortar and pestle, and set aside. Pour the oil for deep-frying into a wok or large saucepan and heat to 350°F, or until bubbles appear up the sides of a wooden chopstick when inserted into the hot oil. Meanwhile, drain the lotus root slices and dry thoroughly on paper towels. Set a wire rack onto a plate and place it near the stove.

Deep-fry the lotus root slices for 3 to 5 minutes—they should be turning golden. Work in batches to stop the temperature of the oil from dropping too much. Remove the chips with a slotted spoon and sprinkle generously with the seasoning before transferring to the wire rack to drain. Let cool and then serve. These will keep for 2 days, sealed in an airtight container.

Mushrooms like shimeji (both brown and white) and enoki are very delicate compared with the more robust shiitake and king oyster mushrooms, and indeed Western closed-cup and cremino varieties. The shimejis have a firm and slightly crunchy texture when cooked, and as such they work well in stir-fried dishes and soups. The brown have a slightly nuttier flavor compared to the white but when I'm selecting which is best for a dish I am often led by esthetics.

STIR-FRIED SHIMEJI *and* KALE *with* BUTTER SOY SAUCE

Wash the mushrooms and slice across the base where the stems clump together. Separate the mushrooms carefully into small clusters using your fingers.

Heat the oil in a wok to just below smoking. Add the kale or other greens and a splash of water. Cover and let steam for a couple of minutes over medium heat, or until the leaves are tender. Remove the lid and stir until any remaining moisture has evaporated. Then push the greens to one side of the wok and turn the heat up to maximum. Immediately add the mushrooms and let sear for 30 seconds. Then, stir the mushrooms, add the butter, and stir-fry everything for another 30 seconds. Add the soy sauce, stir-fry for 30 seconds, and then remove from the heat. Scatter with the snipped chives to garnish, and serve.

1 package of fresh white beech (bunapi) shimeji mushrooms

1 package of fresh brown beech (buna) shimeji mushrooms

1 tablespoon cooking oil

handful of kale, cavolo nero, or collard greens, washed and finely sliced

1½ tablespoons butter

1 tablespoon soy sauce

small bundle of chives, snipped into ½-inch pieces, to garnish

SERVES

2

AS A SIDE DISH

This is a great master teriyaki sauce recipe. Salmon and chicken are particularly good with it, but the meatiness of king oyster mushrooms means that they completely absorb the flavor. Slightly smoky and unexpectedly rich, I don't see this as a vegetarian alternative; it's completely satisfying in its own right.

GRILLED TERIYAKI KING OYSTER MUSHROOMS

Slice the king oyster mushrooms lengthwise ¼inch thick. Lay them out in a dish so that none overlap. Whisk the mirin, soy sauce, sake, and sugar together, then pour evenly over the mushrooms. Let marinate for an hour.

Preheat a ridged cast-iron grill pan over high heat until smoking. Turn the heat down to medium. Shake the marinade from the mushrooms (reserve the marinade), and brush with the cooking oil. Cook in one layer for 3 minutes, then turn 90 degrees so that you get crisscross char marks. Flip the mushrooms over and repeat the process.

Meanwhile, simmer the remaining marinade in a saucepan over medium heat for 30 seconds.

Add the mushrooms to a serving dish and drizzle the remaining marinade over them. Pile the julienned scallion on top and drizzle with the lemon juice.

3 fresh king oyster mushrooms
1 tablespoon mirin
3 tablespoons light soy sauce
3 tablespoons sake
1 teaspoon superfine sugar
1 tablespoon cooking oil
1 scallion, julienned
1 teaspoon lemon juice

SERVES 2

Sriracha is an incredibly popular chili sauce, originally from a province in Thailand. It's one of the milder chili sauces, which might be why it has gained such popularity—it's not going to flame your face off. Thanks to the garlic content, this sauce is best suited to meals post-10 A.M., but really it goes with anything. Make sure you use the large slender chiles, like jalapeño or serrano. Using bird's-eye chiles, for example, would make it inedibly spicy. This makes a small pot's worth, so you may want to double or triple the recipe if you're a real fan of the sauce.

HOMEMADE SRIRACHA

Discard the stems of the chiles and chop the flesh coarsely. Add to a blender with the garlic, sugar, salt, and water and blend to a very fine paste. Place in a clean jar with a loose-fitting lid and let stand in a dark warm place for 3 days (a kitchen cupboard is perfect) so the chiles can start fermenting with the sugar and salt. After a couple of days you'll see bubbles starting to form.

Add the vinegar, and then pour the mixture into a small saucepan and simmer on medium heat for about 15 minutes until it thickens a little. Let cool, then blend again with a hand-held stick blender. Strain through a fine sieve into a bowl to get rid of the pulp and seeds, then spoon into a sterilized glass jar and seal. This will keep in the fridge for up to 1 month, and will thicken on cooling.

¾ lb large red chiles
1 garlic clove, peeled
2 tablespoons dark soft brown sugar
1 tablespoon salt
2 tablespoons water

MAKES

1 SMALL JAR

Pomelo is a beast—it looks like an enormous grapefruit, and I suppose that is essentially what it is; the segments within the fruit are looser and more defined, but it shares that sweet/sour/bitter flavor, perfect for pairing with a rich fish, such as salmon. Look for yellow pomelos to signify ripeness, but, of course, you can use grapefruit in its place.

THAI CRISPY-SKINNED SALMON & POMELO SALAD

SERVES 2

1 salmon fillet, weighing about 8 to 10 oz, skin on

1 teaspoon cooking oil

3½ oz pomelo flesh, broken into small chunks

handful of bean sprouts, blanched and drained

4 red Asian shallots, thinly sliced

½ cucumber, soft insides scooped out and discarded, cut into matchsticks

2 kaffir lime leaves, stems removed, rolled into a cigar shape, and thinly sliced

1 sprig of mint, leaves picked, rolled into a cigar shape, and thinly sliced

a few sprigs of fresh cilantro, coarsely chopped

1 lemon grass stalk, woody outer layers removed

1 bird's-eye chile

juice of 1 lime

2 teaspoons sugar

1 tablespoon fish sauce

Rub the salmon fillet with the oil and place in a cold, nonstick skillet, skin-side down. Slowly bring up to high heat (this makes the skin crispy). Once the skin is sizzling, turn the heat down to medium and check the salmon frequently until it is golden brown and crisp. Flip the salmon fillet over and cook for 30 seconds (or a minute if you have a very thick fillet), and hen remove from the heat and let rest in the skillet.

Combine the pomelo with the bean sprouts, shallots, cucumber, lime leaves, mint, and cilantro in a large mixing bowl.

Slice the lemon grass core into very thin disks, add to a mortar and pound with a pestle a couple of times. Then add the bird's-eye chile and pound a few times more. You want to release the flavor but not pulverize the ingredients. Add the lime juice, sugar, and fish sauce and stir to combine.

Remove the skin from the salmon fillet and set aside, then break the salmon into large chunks with your fingers and add to the salad. Add the dressing, toss through your hands a few times, and then scoop it out into a serving dish. To serve, crack the salmon skin into a few pieces and set it on top.

This is a take on a classic Hong Kong dessert, often served in dim sum restaurants. It's a cold dish, refreshing for a hot day and light enough to eat after a rich meal. The pomelo, especially, gives short sharp bursts of acid, contrasting with the sweetness of the mango. You can buy sweetened mango pulp in cans at Indian grocery stores and in some supermarkets, which is ideal; otherwise, make the pulp from the fresh fruit with a little water and sugar added until it's the consistency of liquid honey.

SAGO WITH POMELO *and* COCONUT

SERVES 4

½ **cup** tapioca pearls

2 tablespoons superfine sugar

⅔ **cup** coconut milk

pinch of salt

1½ cups mango pulp

1 mango, sliced down either side of the seed and flesh cubed

3½ oz pomelo flesh

½ lime, for squeezing

Add the tapioca to a large saucepan filled with plenty of boiling water. Boil, covered, for 10 minutes, stirring a couple of times. Remove from the heat and let stand for another 10 minutes so that it's completely translucent and soft.

Stir the sugar into the coconut milk until dissolved. Drain the tapioca through a sieve and rinse well to get rid of the excess starch. Immediately add it to the coconut milk, along with the salt, stir well, and place in the fridge until you are ready to serve. Don't leave it hanging around in the sieve or it will stick to it.

Add 3 tablespoons of the tapioca mixture to each of 4 small cocktail glasses or glass dessert bowls. Then place 6 tablespoons mango pulp to float on top of each, followed by the diced mango and pomelo flesh. Squeeze a little fresh lime juice over each serving.

1 **large** green unripe mango,
or ½ unripe papaya

½ garlic clove, peeled

small handful of dried shrimps, washed

1 **teaspoon** jaggery (palm sugar), or to taste

juice of ½ lime

2 bird's-eye chiles, or to taste

2 snake beans or 4 green snap beans,
cut into 1¼in pieces

1 **tablespoon** roasted peanuts

1 **to** 2 **tablespoons** fish sauce

5 cherry tomatoes

GREEN MANGO SALAD (SOM TAM)

SERVES 2

If you have wandered around Bangkok at any point, you will be familiar with the rhythmic pounding sound of pestle on mortar, as ladies sit by the roadside making this salad, called som tam, to sell. Som tam is one seriously spicy salad, made by pounding vegetables. Even if you refuse the chiles they hold up at you, there is still enough residual fire in those mortars from previous customers' salads to make a face-melting difference. Unripe mangos or papaya are perfect for it, since they are a little tart but robust enough to deal with the classic pounding action required for this dish. Once your fruit becomes riper, it's best to do something else with it, or it will simply turn to mush.

Peel your mango (or papaya), discard the seed (or seeds), and julienne the flesh (a julienne peeler is a wonderful and inexpensive gadget).

Throw the garlic into a mortar and pound to a paste with a pestle. Add the dried shrimps and give them a pounding. Add the sugar, lime juice, and whole chiles and give them a quick bash. Add the beans, peanuts, and half the julienned mango (or papaya) with 1 tablespoon fish sauce. Give the mixture a good bashing, then mix it together with the rest of the julienned mango (or papaya).

At this point, taste it to see if it needs any more fish sauce or sugar. It should be face-crunchingly spicy. Smash the tomatoes (shield yourself against squirtage) in the mortar, then add to the mango (or papaya) mixture. Serve with some steamed glutinous (sticky) rice.

➳ OTHER IDEAS

If you can't get hold of unripe mango or papaya, try making the salad with a combination of carrot and daikon (Asian radish), or even cucumber.

Tamarind is a tree fruit that's used in cuisines all over the world. Mexicans make it into a drink (tamarindo), which I like with a drop of mezcal in it. The Thais use tamarind in cooking a lot, as do the Indians, and it's also used in Africa, where the tree originates. British Worcestershire and HP sauces contain tamarind, too. It has a specific fruity sourness that is more mellow than citrus.

This is traditionally made with crab in Vietnam, but because I'm a show-off and mainly because I like lobster more, I've used that instead. This is a really messy one; have finger bowls and napkins at the ready.

SERVES 2

LOBSTER IN TAMARIND SAUCE

2½ oz chunk from a block of tamarind with seeds

1¼ cups just-boiled water

1 live lobster, weighing 1¾ to 2¼ lb, placed in the freezer for 20 minutes

2 tablespoons fish sauce

¼ cup jaggery (palm sugar), or to taste

1 tablespoon Shaoxing rice wine

1 tablespoon cooking oil

3 garlic cloves, minced

1 large red chile, coarsely chopped

½ teaspoon ground white pepper

3 scallions, white parts sliced into 3-inch sections, green parts finely sliced

½ tablespoon cornstarch, mixed with **2 tablespoons** cold water

Place the tamarind chunk in a saucepan with the just-boiled water to cover it. Use a fork or spoon to work the tamarind flesh away from the seeds. This will take about 10 minutes. Once the liquid is cool enough, use your fingers to continue to work away the flesh and let it dissolve in the liquid. Strain through a sieve, reserving the water.

Bring a large saucepan of water to a boil. Add the frozen lobster, cover, and boil for 4 minutes. Then remove the lobster and let cool for 10 minutes. Using a dish towel to protect your hands, remove the elastic bands on the lobster's claws. Lay the lobster out on a cutting board, hold the body with one hand, and twist the claws off with the other. Separate the body from the tail by twisting and pulling it apart with your hands. Chop the tail across the width into 3 parts. Using a sharp knife, cut down lengthwise through the head. There will be greenish liquid goo—this is the brains, and perfectly safe to eat. Scoop into a bowl. Chop through the base of the claws, then crack the claws using the base of a sharp knife tapped once just under the lobster claw joint so that the sauce can get to the meat.

Mix the tamarind water, fish sauce, sugar, rice wine, and 2 tablespoons of water together. Heat in a saucepan over medium heat until simmering. Stir for a couple of minutes or so until the sugar dissolves. Taste for the sweet and sour balance, adding more tamarind water if it isn't sour enough, or more sugar if it's too sour. Add the green lobster goo and mix well.

Heat the cooking oil in a wok over medium heat. Add the garlic and chile so that they sizzle, and stir-fry them for 30 seconds. Add the lobster pieces and tamarind mixture. Then add the white pepper and the whites of the scallions, stir, and cover. Simmer, covered, for 3 minutes, stir, and then add the cornstarch solution and simmer for an additional 2 minutes, covered, until the lobster is cooked through and the sauce is glossy. Remove the lid, garnish with the greens of the scallion, and serve with vegetables and steamed rice or slices of baguette to dip in the sauce.

This tart is a classic preparation that has been given an Asian twist with the inclusion of coconut and some of the fruits you'll find at the Asian supermarket. While the tart is pretty, it also allows the flavor of the fruits to come through fairly unadulterated. One thing to note is that for a successful crème pâtissière free from lumps, you must beat the daylights out of it. I speak from experience.

SERVES
8

MANGOSTEEN, DRAGONFRUIT & KIWI TART *with* COCONUT CREAM

For the pastry:
2 cups all-purpose flour, plus extra for dusting
½ cup powdered sugar
pinch of salt
finely grated zest of **1** orange
1 free-range egg yolk, beaten
1 stick cold unsalted butter, cut into cubes
3 tablespoons ice-cold water

For the crème pâtissière:
4 free-range egg yolks
¼ cup superfine sugar
2 tablespoons all-purpose flour
2 tablespoons cornstarch
1½ cups coconut milk

For the topping:
4 strawberries, hulled and finely sliced
1 kiwi fruit, peeled and finely sliced
2 mangosteens, stems removed, then split to remove the globes of white, creamy fruit
1 dragonfruit, halved, flesh scooped out, and sliced
⅓ cup blueberries
2 tablespoons peach or apricot jam
1 tablespoon just-boiled water

Sift the flour and powdered sugar for the pastry into a large mixing bowl, and then stir in the salt and the orange zest. Add the egg yolk and mix well. Add the butter cubes and rub into the flour mixture with your fingers until it resembles bread crumbs. Add 2 tablespoons of the iced water and stir until you get a loose dough; you may not need all of the water. Once the dough comes together, seal it in plastic wrap it and let chill in the fridge for at least half an hour.

For the crème pâtissière, place the egg yolks, sugar, flour, and cornstarch into an electric stand mixer or a large bowl and beat for about 10 minutes, or until smooth, pale, and creamy. Heat the coconut milk in a saucepan until it boils. Then remove it from the heat and let cool for 30 seconds.

Preheat the oven to 400°F. Pour half the coconut milk into the egg and sugar mixture while beating at a high speed for 5 minutes. Pour the mixture back into the saucepan with the rest of the coconut milk over medium heat, beating all the while with a hand-held electic beater. Heat until simmering—at this point it should be thickening rapidly. You want it to resemble a stiff jam. Remove from the heat, let cool for 10 minutes, and then cover with plastic wrap touching the top of the crème pâtissière. Place in a sink full of cold water, but do not let the saucepan float. Let cool completely.

Meanwhile, lightly dust a work surface with flour. Roll your pastry out to ½ inch thick and large enough to line the inside of an 8½-inch tart pan with a removable bottom. Freeze any leftover pastry dough for another time. Carefully press the pastry into the bottom and up the insides of the pan. Place a sheet of nonstick parchment paper into the tart crust and add dried beans to weigh it down. Bake for 15 to 20 minutes, or until browned and crisp. Remove from the oven, lift the paper and beans out of the crust, and transfer to a wire rack to cool.

To assemble, spoon the crème pâtissière into the crust until two-thirds full. Decorate the tart as you wish with the prepared fruit and blueberries. Finally, loosen the jam with the just-boiled water and use the mixture to lightly glaze the fruit and the crust. Let cool before serving.

HOW TO PREPARE PINEAPPLE *the* ASIAN WAY

The pineapple is an interesting fruit, and one of the rare ones that works in both sweet and savory dishes. There's an enzyme in pineapple that tenderizes meat, which is why it sometimes tickles your tongue when you bite into it; it is, effectively, biting you back. If you've ever been to Thailand, the Philippines, or Mexico, you might have been blown away, as I was, by the skill and dexterity with which the street vendors strip a pineapple of its skin and eyes to create chunks of sweet, juicy fruit ready to eat without having to spit anything out or have any of it stuck in your teeth. A few sharp hacks of a large knife (or a machete, but let's stick to a knife) is all it takes.

When choosing your pineapple, give the bottom of the fruit a good sniff. People may look at you askance, but a ripe pineapple will smell so. Also, give the green leaves nearest the center of the fruit a little tug; a ripe fruit will release them easily.

Stand the pineapple upright and, starting 2 inches from the top of the green leaves, slice the skin off close to the flesh to reveal the "eyes" all the way around.

Cut the quarters in half, and then slice out the tough, woody center. It's now ready to eat, or you can cut it into smaller bite-size pieces.

Now take the top and bottom off. Rinse the pineapple, then cut it in half lengthwise and then in half again.

Holding the pineapple with your left hand, you will see that the eyes sit in a diagonal row. Make an incision with your knife at a 45-degree angle from below the outer edge of 2 to 3 of the eyes, and repeat on the upper side so that the eyes come away cleanly. Repeat down the pineapple to the bottom, and then turn the pineapple around and repeat until all the eyes have been cut out. Eventually the starting point will meet the end.

This chile, sugar, and salt dip comes in a little bag with fruit purchased from street vendors in Thailand. It's fantastic with very sweet fruit, but also with acidic fruit like green apples, since the sugar balances things out a little. Green mango, pineapple, cantaloupe, and watermelon work really well with this. Sometimes, for a little variation, I even crush in a few mint leaves.

CHILE SUGAR SALT DIP

1 large red chile
1 tablespoon fine salt
2 tablespoons superfine sugar

Slice the chile in half lengthwise and scoop the seeds out with a teaspoon. Slice thinly into half rings and place in a mortar. Add the salt and sugar and pound lightly with a pestle, tainting the sugar and salt mixture pink.

Durian smells disgusting. It smells like something died in stagnant water while wearing a teenage boy's football socks. Even the fruit itself doesn't look inviting, given the spikes it's covered in. But if you can get past that, it has a wonderfully creamy, custard texture and a fragrance in its flavor, if not smell.

DURIAN ICE CREAM

Remove the flesh from the pieces of durian. There is usually a hard seed in the middle of each piece, which you should discard. Place the fruit in a blender. Add the rest of the ingredients and blend until smooth.

Pour into an ice-cream maker and churn/freeze following manufacturer's directions. Alternatively, pour into a freezer-proof container and freeze for a couple of hours until almost frozen. Blend again to break down the ice crystals, then return it to the freezer. You will have to repeat this process 3 to 4 times until the ice cream freezes smooth.

2 large pieces of durian (you can find this in the fridge or sometimes freezer section of the Asian supermarket)

1½ cups evaporated milk

1 cup heavy whipping cream

⅓ cup superfine sugar

pinch of salt

On many roadsides in Thailand, a roti vendor will be slapping dough out deftly, and chopping fruits or even egg into the dough being cooked on a hot plate for a snack or dessert. Crisp, crunchy pastry with just-warm bananas drizzled with condensed milk is my absolute favorite. Don't worry if you can't quite get the dough-slapping right—practice makes perfect.

MAKES 8

BANANA ROTIS

2 tablespoons superfine sugar

hefty pinch of salt

1 cup warm water

3 tablespoons milk

2 tablespoons unsalted butter, melted

1 large free-range egg

1 lb 2 oz all-purpose flour, sifted, plus extra for dusting

cooking oil, for oiling

3½ tablespoons clarified butter, for cooking

8 ripe bananas

14 fl oz can condensed milk, to serve

To make the dough, dissolve the sugar and salt in the warm water in a large bowl, then add the milk and melted butter.

In a separate small bowl, beat the egg lightly and then add it to the liquid. Add all the sifted flour, then mix well. Knead the dough by hand on a lightly floured work surface (or, use an electric stand mixer fitted with a dough hook) for at least 15 minutes. The dough should be tacky but not sticking to your hand. Set the dough into a lightly oiled bowl. Seal with plastic wrap so that it's in contact with the dough (this prevents it from forming a crust), and let stand to rest for at least 30 minutes.

Lightly oil a clean work surface. Pluck a piece of dough roughly one-eighth of the total and smooth it into a ball by pulling the dough around itself into a spherical shape—this shouldn't take longer than 30 seconds. The ball should be smooth and tight, and about the size of a golf ball. Tuck the rest of the dough in and pinch it together. Then place the dough ball on an oiled cookie sheet. Repeat the process to make 8 equal-sized dough balls.

Flatten a dough ball into a rough circular shape and then gently lift the side closest to you and drag it toward you. Lift quickly but delicately and slap it back onto the work surface. The elasticity and stickiness of the dough means that it shouldn't rip too easily and it should stretch thinly as you drag it. Repeat this process until the dough is roughly $\frac{1}{16}$ to $\frac{1}{8}$ inch thick. The thinner the better, but remember that you have to lift it into a pan. A few holes are fine. Alternatively, you can roll the dough with a rolling pin.

Meanwhile, heat half the clarified butter in a large skillet over medium heat—the butter needs to be really hot in order to crisp the dough, but not burn it. Carefully lift the dough into the pan; it should sizzle. Slice a banana directly onto the center of the roti. Fold the dough into a rectangular shape, flipping the sides in toward the center so they overlap and seal, and then flip it over, adding a little more clarified butter if needed. Fry for about 3 minutes on each side until it is golden brown and crispy on both sides. Repeat this process with the other rotis. To serve, chop each roti into 4 squares and place on a plate, then drizzle with condensed milk.

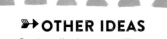

➤ OTHER IDEAS

Replace the banana with chopped-up pineapple (*see page 118*).

Drizzle with melted chocolate instead of condensed milk

Lemon grass is a versatile ingredient that can be used for both savory and sweet dishes. These pears are poached in lemon grass syrup until the flesh is soft and yielding. They can be served either as a dessert with a scoop of vanilla ice cream, or you can chop the pear up and eat it with yogurt for a decadent breakfast.

POACHED PEARS IN LEMON GRASS SYRUP

SERVES
2

Peel the pears and leave whole, with a bit of stalk. Take a saucepan large enough to hold the 2 pears, add the honey, lemon juice, lemon grass, water, and ginger and bring to a simmer on medium heat. Add the pears and simmer gently, uncovered, on low heat, for 30 minutes. Turn the pears once halfway through. Then insert a knife into a pear—it should be tender. If not, simmer for a little while longer.

Remove the pears, then turn the heat up to reduce the syrup by one third. Strain the syrup through a fine sieve into a bowl and let cool for 20 minutes. Return the pears to the syrup and let cool completely.

To serve, place a pear on each plate and drizzle with a little of the syrup.

2 pears
3 tablespoons liquid honey
juice of **½** lemon
2 lemon grass stalks, minced
2½ cups water
1 thin slice of fresh ginger root, peeled
1 tablespoon superfine sugar

CHAPTER

FRIDGE & FREEZER

FRIDGE & FREEZER

The fridge and freezer sections of most Asian supermarkets are not like those of their Western counterparts. In addition to the basic raw ingredients you would expect to find in the West, they stock items that most people don't have the time or the expertise to make from scratch at home. I've included interesting cuts of meat that you usually come across in Asian supermarkets, and even on restaurant menus, but I've given alternatives in case you find them too challenging to bear.

(1) TOFU (BEAN CURD)

Fresh forms of tofu are a big part of Asian cuisines. Besides the marinated, egg (*see page 135*), or deep-fried versions (tofu puffs), these are sold in cartons in water to keep them fresh. They range from extra-soft silken tofu, generally used for soups and sauces, to extra-firm tofu, which has the structure to stand up to stir-frying. Dispel any previously formed ideas (if you had them) that tofu is vegetarian food, used to replace meat, because it isn't so. It's a texture in its own right with a delicate flavor and often cooked with meat.

(2 & 3) DUMPLING WRAPPERS (SKINS)

While you can make your own potsticker wrappers (2), which are of a better quality than ready-made, the ones you can buy in the fridge or freezer are still worth using if you're short of time or low on energy. Wonton wrappers (3), however, are best left to the professionals and these can be purchased either ready to use from the fridge or ready to defrost from the freezer.

(4) KIMCHI

Kimchi is from Korea and hundreds of different versions are available. This is a method of preserving vegetables, and although the most common is made with cabbage, you can apply the kimchi treatment to almost any vegetable. The classic, Chinese cabbage (Chinese leaf or Napa cabbage), is rubbed with a glutinous rice flour paste to encourage fermentation, along with an eye-watering amount of chili powder, garlic, and other bits and pieces. Very traditional recipes use raw oysters in the mixture too, which, given how long this stuff can sit in your fridge, is frankly terrifying. Deliciously terrifying. Most Asian supermarkets will have at least the cabbage style in the fridge; for the more adventurous types, I've included a recipe to make your own at home (*see page 143*).

1.

4.

2.

3.

(5 & 6) FISH CAKES, FISHBALLS & FISH PASTE

Japanese fish cakes, called kamaboko, are a riot of colors and shapes. Some are decorated as cartoon characters, while others include pink swirls and other-worldly colors one might not be so used to eating. In most Asian supermarkets, the kinds of fish cakes (5) and fishballs (6) on offer are far more restrained and usually limited in range to different flavorings and preparation; some are fried before being packaged, others simply steamed. You can also buy the fish paste itself to shape whichever way you choose, and this is usually found in the fridge or freezer. I've tried (several times) to make my own fishballs at home, but they are just not as good as ready-made. It's something to do with the type of fish that's used, which isn't available in the West; there's a certain kind of protein in this particular fish that, when you break the flesh down and pound it repeatedly, produces that characteristic bouncy texture. I always have a package in the fridge to add to stir-fried dishes or noodle soups.

OFFAL

There's no denying it—Asians are probably among the more adventurous when it comes to the palate. In fact, they redefine nose-to-tail eating. I remember the haunted look in my friend's eye, followed by a shiver, as he recounted his vacation in Japan, during which he was served cod's sperm. I won't inflict bodily fluids on you, but chicken's feet, tendon, and tripe are all worth trying.

5.

6.

The classic Cantonese wonton contains pork and shrimp, which makes it lighter; perfect for bobbing around in a noodle soup. This Sichuanese version is meatier and a little denser to stand up to the wallop of the spicy, lip-tingling chili dressing.

SICHUAN WONTONS

For the wontons:

4 dried shiitake mushrooms, soaked in just-boiled water for 30 minutes, then drained and stems discarded

1 lb ground pork—you want a little fat in this, so ask your butcher for it

3½ oz soft silken tofu, drained well

1 teaspoon peeled and grated fresh ginger root

3 scallions, minced

½ teaspoon ground white pepper

1 teaspoon sesame oil

1 teaspoon oyster sauce

½ teaspoon salt

1 package fresh wonton wrappers / skins (cover them with a damp dish towel to prevent them from drying out when not in use)

all-purpose flour, for dusting

For the sauce:

⅓ cup chili oil with sediment (*see page 12*)

¼ cup light soy sauce

1 tablespoon Chinkiang black vinegar

1 teaspoon sesame oil

2 teaspoons sugar

2 teaspoons minced garlic

1 scallion, diagonally sliced, to garnish

For the wontons, chop the mushrooms finely and mix with the pork in a large bowl. Break the tofu into chunks and add to the pork. Add all the other ingredients, except the wrappers and flour, and stir thoroughly with chopsticks until they have all combined well.

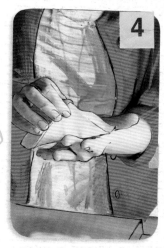

Take a wonton wrapper in your hand and place a corner pointing to your wrist. Add a scant tablespoon of filling to the center.

Wet the top left- and right-hand edges with a finger dipped in water.

Bring the bottom edges up to meet the wet edges, and press to make a triangle.

Place on a floured plate and repeat until all the filling has been used up. Leftover wrappers should be wrapped well and frozen.

Bring the bottom 2 points to meet around the front, wetting one edge to seal it.

Gently squeeze the air out of the area around the filling and seal well.

You can freeze the wontons on a floured baking pan and combine in a freezer bag once frozen, then cook from frozen. Cook in a large saucepan of gently simmering water for 5 to 6 minutes (or 10 minutes if cooking from frozen) until they rise up and bob on the surface and are cooked through.

To make the sauce, combine the chili oil, soy sauce, vinegar, sesame oil, and sugar in a bowl. Mix well until all is incorporated, then stir in the garlic.

When the wontons are cooked, drain them well and combine with the sauce. Scatter the sliced scallion on top as a garnish.

For a lighter, more summery dumpling filling, I like to use a higher ratio of shrimp to pork. You still need the pork in there for juiciness and flavor, but this becomes more of a background binding agent. You can use any green spring vegetable, like fava beans, watercress, or peas. If you are using any vegetables that might give off moisture when cooked such as watercress or spinach, give them a quick blanch and squeeze dry before adding them to the mixture.

MAKES ABOUT

SHRIMP, ASPARAGUS & WILD GARLIC POTSTICKERS

18

5½ oz raw peeled shrimp

1 tablespoon baking soda mixed with **2 tablespoons** cold water (optional)

3½ oz fatty ground pork

3 scallions, finely sliced

1½ teaspoons peeled and minced fresh ginger root

1 tablespoon light soy sauce

½ teaspoon salt

½ teaspoon sesame oil

pinch of ground white pepper

4½ oz asparagus spears, trimmed of woody ends

1¾ oz wild garlic leaves

1 teaspoon cornstarch, plus **1 teaspoon** mixed with **2 teaspoons** cold water

1 package round white dumpling wrappers / skins / gyoza (cover them with a damp dish towel to prevent them from drying out when not in use)

all-purpose flour, for dusting

2 tablespoons vegetable oil, plus a little extra for frying a sample of the filling to check the seasoning

For the dipping sauce:

3 tablespoons Chinkiang black vinegar or, if you can't find it, **2 tablespoons** balsamic vinegar with **1 teaspoon** sherry vinegar

1-inch piece of fresh ginger root, peeled and cut into fine julienne

1 red chile, minced (optional)—reserve half for garnish

This part is optional, but it makes the shrimp extra juicy with an almost-crunchy texture: chop the shrimp roughly and let marinate in the baking soda solution while you prepare your other ingredients.

Add the pork, scallions, ginger, soy sauce, salt, sesame oil, and the white pepper to a large mixing bowl. Slice the asparagus spears into disks ½-inch thick, reserving the tips for garnish, and mince the wild garlic. Add both ingredients to the bowl. Drain the shrimp, pat dry with paper towels, and add to the pork mixture. Use your hands to really get in there and make sure all the ingredients are mixed well and evenly distributed. Finally, add the dry cornstarch and mix briefly again.

At this point, it's a good idea to fry a tablespoon of the pork mixture in a little vegetable oil in a nonstick skillet and taste it to check the seasoning.

Fold the wrapper in half over the filling, pinching to seal the center point.

Take a dumpling wrapper in your hand and place a tablespoon of the filling in the center. Wet the edge of one half of the wrapper with a little of the cornstarch paste to help it stick.

Fold 3 pleats in each half to enclose the filling in the pouch, using your middle finger to bring the pastry around, with your thumb behind, to form the pleat.

05 Place on a floured plate, bottom down, so that the bottom flattens. Repeat until all the filling is used up. (Leftover wrappers should be wrapped well and frozen.) At this point you can freeze the dumplings on a floured baking pan (provided your shrimp or meat were not previously frozen). Then, once frozen, add the dumplings to a resealable freezer bag. Cook from frozen (don't defrost them first.)

If cooking immediately, set a nonstick skillet on medium heat and add the vegetable oil. Set the dumplings carefully into the oil and fry for about 3 minutes until the bottoms have browned. Add a few splashes of water and put a lid on so that the tops of the dumplings steam. The water may evaporate. If so, add a splash more so that you've steamed them for 5 minutes. Remove the lid; there shouldn't be much water left at this point; if there is, cook with the lid off until it has evaporated, and add a drizzle of oil. Check the bottoms, which should be nicely bronzed.

Meanwhile, combine the dipping sauce ingredients in a small dish and serve on a platter, garnished with the asparagus tips, sliced in half and scattered on top, along with the reserved red chile, if using. Serve the dumplings on a plate, upended to show off their lovely bronzed bottoms.

Give it a squeeze at the end to ensure it is sealed. Alternatively, bring the other half of the wrapper up to meet the wet half and use the tines of a fork to seal, pressing any air out.

When I was a kid, I would make these with my mom and sister, a little production line of wrapping and folding, until we had hundreds of dumplings. Wontons are incredibly versatile; you can fill them with almost anything, as long as it doesn't release too much water. There are many ways of folding dumplings, but the one I've detailed here is the simplest.

25

CLASSIC DEEP-FRIED WONTONS

3½ oz fatty ground pork

2½ oz raw peeled shrimp, coarsely chopped

2 scallions, minced

3 to 4 dried shiitake mushrooms, soaked in just-boiled water for 30 minutes and then drained and diced, stems discarded

1-inch piece of fresh ginger root, peeled and minced

1½ tablespoons oyster sauce

large pinch of ground white pepper

1 teaspoon light soy sauce

1 tablespoon cornstarch

1 packet fresh wonton wrappers / skins (keep them covered with a damp dish towel to prevent them from drying out when not in use)

all-purpose flour, for dusting

vegetable oil, for deep-frying (optional)

Thoroughly mix all the ingredients, except the wrappers, flour, and oil, together in a bowl. Let stand for about 15 minutes.

Take a wonton wrapper in your hand and place a corner pointing to your wrist. Place a scant tablespoon of filling in the center. Wet the top left- and right-hand edges with a finger dipped in water. Bring the bottom edges up to meet the wet edges, and press to make a triangle. Gently squeeze the air out of the area around the filling and seal well. Bring the bottom 2 points to meet around the front, wetting one edge to seal it. Place on a floured plate and repeat until all the filling is used up. Leftover wrappers should be wrapped well and frozen.

To cook, simmer gently in a large saucepan of water for 5 to 6 minutes (or 10 minutes if using them from frozen), or until they rise to the surface and are cooked through. If serving in a soup, don't cook them in soup stock, because the flour dusting on the wrappers will make it cloudy. Drain from the water and add to stock with or without noodles.

Alternatively, add enough oil to cover the wontons to a wok or large saucepan. Place on high heat and heat to 350°F, or until bubbles appear up the sides of a wooden chopstick when inserted into the hot oil. Fry, in batches, for 4 to 5 minutes. Remove and drain on paper towels, then serve with sweet chili sauce.

Egg tofu is a type of flavored silken tofu (bean curd) usually sold in tubes. It's made by adding eggs to the soy milk before the coagulant is added, and the whole thing is then cooked together so that the egg flavor is incorporated and the tofu takes on a yellow color. Because it's incredibly delicate in texture, you must be careful when handling it. This tofu works really well dusted with flour and fried, and also braised afterward, especially if you have issues with soft tofu's gelatinous texture. I particularly love the way the crispy crust becomes softer under the sauce of this dish, while retaining a little texture contrast.

BRAISED EGG TOFU *with* PORK *and* EGGPLANT

SERVES 4

3 tablespoons cooking oil, divided

2 slim Asian eggplants or **1** medium-sized eggplant, diced into large cubes

1 small tube of egg tofu

⅓ cup cornstarch, for dusting

3 garlic cloves, minced

1 teaspoon peeled and minced fresh ginger

1 large red chile, sliced into thin rings

3½ oz ground pork

1¾ cups chicken stock

2 tablespoons oyster sauce

1 tablespoon light soy sauce

1 teaspoon dark soy sauce

1 teaspoon superfine sugar

1 teaspoon Chinkiang black vinegar

1 scallion, thinly sliced into disks, white and green parts separated

1 teaspoon cornstarch, mixed with **1 tablespoon** cold water

few sprigs of fresh cilantro, to garnish

Heat up 1 tablespoon of the oil in a wok or a nonstick skillet over high heat and stir-fry the eggplant cubes for 3 to 5 minutes, or until the cubes take on some color and become golden. Remove and place on a plate lined with paper towels.

Slice through the tube of the egg tofu in the center with a sharp knife. Gently coax the egg tofu cylinders out of the plastic and carefully onto a separate plate. Slice into disks as thick as your forefinger, then pat dry with paper towels. Heat another tablespoon of oil in the skillet over medium heat, dust each disk of egg tofu in cornstarch, and place in the oil. Fry for 3 minutes on medium heat until one side has taken on a golden brown color, then flip it over and repeat. Remove and place on another plate lined with paper towels. Repeat with the rest of the egg tofu disks.

Heat up the last tablespoon of oil in a large saucepan, clay pot (*see page 11*), or wok over medium heat and fry the garlic, ginger, and chile for 30 seconds or so until fragrant. Add the pork and stir-fry, amalgamating the garlic, ginger, and chile as you go, until the pork has taken on some golden color. Return the eggplant to the mixture, stir to combine, then add the stock, oyster sauce, soy sauces, and sugar. Stir again to combine, then stir in the black vinegar. Add the tofu on top and carefully mix with a spoon so that the disks drop into the liquid—it's OK if they aren't completely submerged.

Cover and braise for 5 minutes, then give it another gentle stir and braise for an additional 5 minutes. Throw in the whites of the scallion and the cornstarch and water mixture and simmer for a couple of minutes to thicken. If using a clay pot, serve at the table, otherwise spoon out into a warmed serving bowl and garnish with the cilantro and the scallion greens. Serve with rice.

➥ OTHER IDEAS

Steam egg tofu with chopped-up shrimp, chicken, and a little soy sauce, or dip in tempura batter, deep-fry, and serve with a sweet chili dip.

Soft tofu (bean curd) is almost like jelly in texture—you have to be quite careful with it so that it doesn't disintegrate on contact with your hands. This dish has been likened to a savory panna cotta—you can dress firmer tofu with this spicy and tangy dressing, but I love the smooth, silky texture contrast with the crunchy peanuts.

STEAMED TOFU *with* SOY, SCALLION & CHILI

SERVES 4 AS A SIDE DISH

Drain the tofu and carefully place it on a plate. Steam in a metal or bamboo steamer over medium heat for 15 minutes.

Meanwhile, heat the cooking oil in a wok on low heat and fry the garlic for 30 seconds, being careful not to burn it. Drain the garlic and place in a bowl.

Combine the soy sauces with the vinegar, sugar, chili oil, oyster sauce, and water and mix well, then carefully pour over the freshly steamed tofu. Garnish with the preserved vegetable, cilantro, scallion, Sichuan pepper, and peanuts. Serve warm, with rice.

1 package (10½ oz or 11¾ oz) soft (not extra-soft) silken tofu (bean curd)

1 tablespoon cooking oil

2 garlic cloves, minced

2 tablespoons light soy sauce

½ teaspoon dark soy sauce

1 teaspoon Chinkiang black vinegar

1 teaspoon superfine sugar

3 tablespoons chili oil (2 of the oil, 1 with sediment—*see page 12*)

1½ tablespoons oyster sauce

1 teaspoon water

2 teaspoons Tianjin preserved vegetable (*see page 162*), well rinsed

small handful of fresh cilantro, coarsely chopped

1 scallion, thinly sliced diagonally

½ teaspoon Sichuan peppercorns, toasted and finely ground

2 tablespoons unsalted roasted peanuts, coarsely chopped

The combination of salt, pepper(s), sugar, and chile makes an addictive, crisp coating for the tofu cubes, yielding to the soft, silky insides. Perfect as a snack with beer, or a side. This coating works wonderfully with squid, too. Simply cut the squid into rings and fry for a shorter length of time; just a minute or two.

SALT *and* PEPPER TOFU

SERVES 4 AS A SIDE DISH

1 block (about 11¼ oz) firm tofu

cooking oil, for deep-frying

cornstarch, for dusting

1 teaspoon ground white pepper

½ teaspoon Sichuan peppercorns, toasted and finely ground

1 teaspoon sugar

1 teaspoon salt flakes

3 garlic cloves, minced

3 large chiles, red and green, thinly sliced into rings—use bird's-eye chiles if you prefer them hotter

2 large scallions, halved lengthwise and sliced into 1-inch pieces

few sprigs of fresh cilantro

wedge of lime

Pat the tofu dry with paper, then cut into ½-inch cubes.

Pour 1½ inches of oil into a wok or saucepan over high heat and heat to 350°F, or until bubbles appear up the sides of a wooden chopstick when inserted into the hot oil. Dust the tofu cubes in the cornstarch, then slip them, 5 or 6 at a time, into the oil. Gently stir them with chopsticks or a metal spatula to prevent them from sticking. They should be crisp and golden after about 5 minutes. Remove with a slotted spoon and drain on paper towels. Return the oil to temperature before frying another batch.

While the tofu is frying, mix the 2 peppers, sugar, and salt together in a small bowl.

When all the tofu cubes have been deep-fried and left to drain, discard all but 2 tablespoons of the oil from the wok or saucepan and reheat it over high heat. Add the garlic, chile rings, and scallions and stir-fry for about 15 seconds, or until fragrant.

Add the tofu and sprinkle in the ground seasonings as you are cooking it. Cook for 1 to 2 minutes, or until golden, stirring constantly to allow the tofu to absorb the flavors. Transfer the tofu, along with all the little pieces left behind, to a plate. Serve immediately, garnished with a few cilantro sprigs and a lime wedge.

This is my take on a traditional Malaysian rojak salad. The amount of fruit in the salad as a savory dish might make you suspicious, but the peanut and shrimp paste sauce balances out the sweet aspect. Deep-fried tofu puffs are excellent here; they soak up the sauce nicely and yield a wonderfully soft texture against the crunch of the vegetables and fruit. Hae ko is yet another shrimp paste, made with sugar, but this type is essential in dishes like this, and also in the famous Penang assam laksa, a hot and sour fish soup. Serve with wooden skewers for people to stab at the salad, in traditional hawker style.

SPICY PEANUT and TOFU PUFF SALAD

Juice the limes into a bowl and add the red onion. This should cover the pieces, but if not, top off with a little water. Let stand for 30 minutes.

Using 2 Chinese spoons stacked with a tofu puff in between, squeeze the excess water out of them. Chop into quarters and add to a large bowl. Add the pear, pineapple, cucumber, apple, daikon, and bean sprouts.

Pound the peanuts using a mortar and pestle until quite fine, then remove from the mortar and set aside. Add the hae ko shrimp paste with the sugar, peanut butter, and sriracha to the mortar and pound the ingredients a few times until all are incorporated. The mixture will be very sticky at this point, so keep working it. Add the tamarind paste and soy sauce and mix well. Really get in there and give it a good stir—it'll be quite thick.

Drain the red onion and give the pieces a rinse, then drain again. Add to the salad, then pour all the dressing in. Mix really well—this may take 5 minutes of tossing and mixing. Scatter with the crushed peanuts, give it another stir, and then serve immediately.

2 limes

1 small red onion, coarsely chopped

6 tofu puffs (see page 128), soaked in just-boiled water for 10 minutes, then drained

1 Asian pear, cored and chopped into bite-size chunks

½ pineapple, peeled, cored, and cut into bite-size chunks (see page 118)

½ cucumber, seeded and chopped into chunks

1 Granny Smith apple, cored and chopped into bite-size chunks

1¾ oz daikon (Asian radish), peeled and chopped into small chunks

large handful of bean sprouts, blanched in boiling water for 30 seconds, then drained

⅔ cup unsalted peanuts, toasted

2 tablespoons hae ko (also called petis udang—see page 17)

2 tablespoons jaggery (palm sugar)

1 tablespoon smooth peanut butter

1 tablespoon sriracha (see page 109 for homemade, or use ready-made)

½ tablespoon tamarind paste

2 tablespoons light soy sauce

Marinated tofu (bean curd) is usually found in the fridge section of the Asian supermarket, and takes the hassle out of flavoring the tofu yourself. Invariably marinated in five-spice powder or chile and sesame, it's the ideal weeknight staple for a stir-fried dish, and you can rustle this one up in less than half an hour. It's bright and perky, and leftovers are also great cold as a salad. You can vary the vegetables, but to keep it visually interesting, try to get a good mixture of colors, and cut everything to the same sort of shape.

MARINATED TOFU & FIVE VEGETABLE STIR-FRY

SERVES
2

1 tablespoon cooking oil

1-inch piece of fresh ginger root, peeled and minced

2 garlic cloves, minced

1 small carrot, sliced into 1½-inch sticks

1 small zucchini, sliced into 1½-inch sticks

handful of green or purple kale, coarsely chopped

2 purple cabbage leaves, finely sliced

3½ oz marinated tofu (bean curd), chopped into bite-size pieces

1 scallion, white parts cut into 1¼-inch lengths, green parts finely sliced into rings

1¾ oz fine green snap beans or sugar snap peas

2 tablespoons light soy sauce

handful of fresh cilantro, coarsely chopped

Heat your wok with the oil over medium heat. Swirl the wok around to coat the inside with the hot oil. Add the ginger and garlic and fry for 30 seconds, then add the carrot and zucchini and stir-fry for 2 to 3 minutes, or until they start to become tender. Turn the heat up to high and add the kale and the purple cabbage. Add a splash of water and stir-fry the vegetables until the water has evaporated, then add the tofu and another splash of water, and stir-fry again. Add the whites of the scallion and the green snap beans or sugar snap peas and repeat the stir-frying process with another splash of water. Add the soy sauce and stir to combine, then add the scallion greens and cilantro and remove the pan from the heat.

Serve with rice, or add cooked rice vermicelli noodles just after the green snap beans or sugar snap peas, along with the soy sauce, for a noodle dish.

This stuff is dangerous. The first time I made it, I excitedly got the jar out of the cupboard to give it its first taste test. There were bubbles going up the side of the jar and a light fizzing noise could be heard emanating from it. I released the latch of the clip-top jar and the contents exploded up the wall. My roommate screamed. My kitchen smelled of fermented cabbage for a week. So don't overfill the jar; just use a second jar. Some people add raw oysters or salted shrimp to kimchi, but I'm too much of a coward. Next time, next time...

CABBAGE KIMCHI

MAKES

1 TO 2 JARS

Chop the Chinese cabbage into even-sized pieces. Wash thoroughly, then coat liberally in salt, place in a colander over a bowl or the sink, and let stand for 3 hours, turning every 30 minutes or so. This is so that the salt leaches the moisture from the cabbage.

Beat the water and the glutinous rice flour together in a saucepan over medium heat and bring slowly to a boil, stirring constantly. Cook for a few minutes, then remove from the heat. Let cool.

Stir in the chili powder, then add the garlic, onion, ginger, and apple. Add the fish sauce and mix well.

Wash the cabbage thoroughly, at least a few times, to make sure all the salt has been rinsed off. Drain well, and add to a large bowl. Toss in the scallions, and then add the chili sludge. Combine well using your hands. If you have any broken skin on your hands, wear gloves or it will sting.

Pack into a sterilized jar, leaving plenty of room at the top of the kimchi to allow space for the fermentation gases. Let stand for a day or two, opening the lid every so often to let the gas escape, and then transfer it to the fridge. It's good to eat just as it comes for at least 3 weeks. After that it may become quite strong, but it's still fine to use in stews, stir-fries, and other hot dishes.

2 heads of Chinese cabbage (Chinese leaf or Napa cabbage)

loads of table salt

1 cup water

⅓ cup glutinous rice flour

1 cup coarse Korean chili powder

6 garlic cloves, minced

1 large onion, minced

2-inch piece of fresh ginger root, peeled and grated

2 apples, peeled, cored, and grated

½ cup fish sauce

bunch of scallions, chopped into thirds

"Bread and cheese" doesn't sound very Asian but when you think about it, really, it makes sense, because this is one of those "fusion" recipes. Kimchi is basically a type of pickle, and what goes better in a toasted cheese sandwich? Yup. Pickle. Strangely, the stronger cheeses work well with this; you might assume they would clash, but actually the robust flavors meld together well.

KIMCHI TOASTED CHEESE SANDWICH

MAKES **1**

Butter both sides of one slice of bread and place in a nonstick skillet to assemble. Pile with half the cheese, then drape kimchi on top, pile on the rest of the cheese, and carefully press the other slice of bread on top. Butter the exposed side of the top slice.

Heat the skillet gently to medium heat and place a heavy heatproof object, or another skillet, on top of the sandwich to press it down. Add the cooking oil to the pan to assist the browning process a little. When the cheese on the bottom half looks like it's good and melted, check the underside for browning—it should be a deep golden color. Flip the sandwich over carefully, then place the heavy object on top of the other side and cook for another 5 minutes, checking a few times until the other underside is browned.

Remove from the heat, slice the sandwich in half, and wait a few minutes before devouring—the cheese has a tendency to turn into molten lava.

spreadable butter

2 slices of sturdy bread, such as sourdough

handful of coarsely shredded sharp Cheddar cheese, or a 50:50 mix of Cheddar and Stilton

2 tablespoons Cabbage Kimchi (*see page 143 for homemade*), drained of juice and patted dry with paper towels

1 teaspoon cooking oil

This recipe uses slightly older kimchi—so, kimchi that's sat in the fridge for a while—to get a stronger flavor. If you have bought or made it fresh though, it will still work; just add a little more. This stew is so comforting that in colder weather I eat it at least once a week. The soft tofu has a texture almost like panna cotta, while the egg, having poached in the broth, enriches it and makes it filling, like a big spicy hug.

KIMCHI STEW

SERVES 1

To make the broth, heat the water with the kombu and dried anchovies until simmering. Remove from the heat and add the bonito flakes. Let stand for 15 minutes, and then strain.

Heat the sesame oil in a dolsot (stone bowl—see page 11) or a saucepan and fry the garlic in the oil for a few minutes. Add the gochujang, the fresh chile, if using, and the kimchi, then add the dashi broth and soy sauce. Simmer for 25 minutes, then add the tofu and simmer for another 5 minutes. Break the egg into the stew and simmer for another 3 minutes—if you're using a clay pot you can remove this from the heat immediately and the egg will cook in the residual heat. Top with the scallion and then transfer to a cutting board or heatproof mat. Serve with a bowl of steamed rice.

1 teaspoon sesame oil

1 teaspoon minced garlic

2 teaspoons gochujang (see page 16)

1 small red chile, minced (optional; add if you're a chile head)

3 tablespoons Cabbage Kimchi (see page 143 for homemade), plus 1 tablespoon kimchi juice

1 teaspoon light soy sauce

7 oz soft silken tofu (bean curd), drained, patted dry with paper towels

1 free-range egg

1 scallion, finely sliced diagonally

For the broth:

1¼ cups water

3-inch square of dried kombu (see page 188)

4 dried anchovies, heads removed

small handful of dried bonito flakes (see page 209)

(or substitute all the above with **1¼ cups** ready-made dashi stock)

This is one of those classic Chinese takeout dishes, usually ordered with a load of egg rolls and some sweet and sour pork balls for a calorific and grease-laden start to a meal. It doesn't have to be though; while most takeouts deep-fry this, you can also shallow-fry it to retain some semblance of healthiness. The big bags of uncooked shrimp you can buy at the supermarket are perfect for this—you just need shrimp meat and no shell.

SESAME SHRIMP TOAST

SERVES 2 TO 3 AS AN APPETIZER

Using a rolling pin, roll the slices of bread to flatten them to half their thickness.

Pulse the shrimp in a food processor with the scallion, cilantro, ginger, cornstarch, soy sauce, white pepper, and salt until you have a coarse paste. Stir in the diced water chestnuts.

Smear the shrimp mixture onto one side of the bread slices. Spread the sesame seeds out onto a plate and gently press the shrimp side of the bread down onto the seeds to make them stick.

Heat up the cooking oil in a nonstick skillet over medium heat. Add the bread slices, sesame seed-side down, and fry for 2 to 3 minutes, being careful not to burn the seeds. Flip over carefully and fry for another 2 to 3 minutes until browned and crisp.

Drain on a piece of paper towel, then cut each slice into 4 pieces and serve with sriracha (*see page 109 for homemade, or use ready-made*) or sweet chili dipping sauce.

2 to 3 slices of stale white bread

5½ oz raw peeled shrimp, defrosted if frozen

1 scallion, minced

2 sprigs of fresh cilantro, minced

1-inch piece of fresh ginger root, peeled and minced

1 teaspoon cornstarch

1 teaspoon light soy sauce

pinch of ground white pepper

pinch of salt

3 canned water chestnuts, drained and finely diced

¼ cup white sesame seeds

3 tablespoons cooking oil

Thai holy basil differs from its Italian counterpart in that the leaves are sturdier and tinged with purple. Flavorwise, Italian (or sweet) basil is sweeter and milder, while Thai basil has a stronger aniseed note. Either can be used in this dish, though you should increase the quantity of Italian basil for a stronger flavor.

SHRIMP *with* THAI BASIL

2 tablespoons fish sauce

1 tablespoon oyster sauce

1 teaspoon superfine sugar

pinch of ground white pepper

1 tablespoon cooking oil

8 garlic cloves, minced

1 large red chile, thickly sliced into rings

1 small white onion, thinly sliced into half-moons

½ cup sugar snap peas or snow peas, cut in half

10 raw peeled jumbo shrimp

2 small ripe tomatoes, quartered

small handful of Thai basil, or a hefty handful of Italian basil, leaves plucked from the stems

juice of ½ lime

Combine the fish sauce, oyster sauce, sugar, and white pepper with 1 tablespoon water in a bowl.

Heat the oil in a wok on medium heat, add the garlic, and fry gently for 3 to 4 minutes. Then add the chile rings and stir to combine.

Add the half-moons of onion, then turn the heat up to high and stir-fry for 1 minute, making sure that the garlic doesn't burn. Add the sugar snap peas or snow peas and 3 tablespoons of water, then stir-fry continuously until the water has evaporated. Still on the highest heat, add the shrimp and stir-fry for 1 minute. Then add the tomatoes, basil, and the sauce ingredients, and stir-fry continuously, shaking the pan once or twice, until the shrimp have turned pink.

Remove the pan from the heat and add the lime juice. Serve with rice or noodles.

Soft-shell crabs are something of a rarity in normal supermarkets and at fish dealers, but you can often find them in Asian supermarkets in the freezer section. They are best entombed in a carapace of batter for that crisp contrast to the softness of the crab meat and, although they are not cheap, they make an impressive impact; they look almost prehistoric in this burger, with their legs hanging out of the bun. If you can't find them, then raw peeled jumbo shrimp are a great substitute. It's a messy business eating this thing, but then most burgers are.

MAKES
6
BURGERS

TEMPURA SOFT-SHELL CRAB BURGERS

Tempura is a Japanese method of coating vegetables, meat, or fish in a crisp, light, and greaseless batter. The key to getting it right is to make sure everything is as cold as you can get it, and that it's not left hanging around. Tempura waits for no one.

Use store-bought brioche buns if you can find them, or make your own as follows. These are also great with traditional hamburger buns

For the buns:

2 tablespoons milk, warmed

1¼ cups water

2½ tablespoons sugar

¼ oz sachet dried active yeast

1 lb bread flour, plus extra for dusting

1¼ cups all-purpose flour

1½ teaspoons salt

2 tablespoons butter, diced

1 free-range egg, beaten

1 free-range egg yolk beaten with 1 tablespoon milk, for glazing

white sesame seeds, for sprinkling

For the burgers:

1½ cups all-purpose flour

2 tablespoons cornstarch

1 teaspoon salt

6 soft-shell crabs, defrosted overnight in the fridge, or 6 raw jumbo shrimp per person

2½ cups cooking oil

1¾ cups ice-cold sparkling water

For the accompaniments:

¼ cup sriracha *(see page 109 for homemade, or use ready-made)*, mixed well into ½ cup mayonnaise and 1 tablespoon lemon juice

1 red onion, halved, thinly sliced and soaked in cold water for 20 minutes

Pickled Daikon *(see page 157)* or store-bought gherkins

4 Little Gem lettuce leaves, finely shredded

To make the buns, add the warm milk, water, sugar, and yeast to a small bowl and give the ingredients a good stir. Meanwhile, add the 2 flours and salt to a separate bowl and rub in the butter to create a crumbly texture. Add the beaten whole egg, then stir in the yeast mixture. Combine well. Knead by hand on a lightly floured work surface, or using an electric stand mixer fitted with a dough hook, for 10 minutes, or until it's nice and smooth. Put it back into the bowl, cover it with plastic wrap, and let rise in a warm place for an hour, or until double the size.

Divide the dough into 6 and roll each into a large burger bun shape. Place on a cookie sheet lined with nonstick parchment paper, leaving enough room between them to expand while cooking. Let stand for an hour. Meanwhile, preheat the oven to 400°F.

Glaze the buns with the egg yolk and milk mixture and sprinkle with sesame seeds. Place a tray of water on the bottom rack of the oven, then bake the buns for 15 minutes on the middle rack. Remove from the oven and let cool on a wire rack.

Preheat the oven to 225°F. For the tempura, sift the flour into a bowl with the cornstarch and salt. Refrigerate the flour mixture for at least half an hour before you use it. Drain the defrosted soft-shell crabs and pat dry with paper towels. Pour the oil for deep-frying into a wok or large saucepan and heat to 375°F, or until a bread crumb dropped in sizzles heartily. Just before you are due to use the flour mixture, add the sparkling water and mix briefly with chopsticks—it's OK if it's lumpy—then immediately coat each crab with the batter. Drop them, 1 or 2 at a time, into the hot oil and fry for 4 to 6 minutes, or until browned and crisp. Transfer to a wire rack in the preheated oven while you cook the rest.

To assemble, halve a burger bun and smear the sriracha mayonnaise on both cut sides of the bun halves. Place the half-moons of red onion, a couple slices of pickle, and a little of the shredded lettuce on the bottom bun. Place the soft-shell crab inside and top with the lid. You may need to press the burger down a little so that it all melds together properly. Do the same with the rest of the buns and crabs.

If you wanted to, you could grind your own spices and make a deep, rich, aromatic curry sauce for this, but that's not really in keeping with the nature of the dish. Bouncy fishballs in a sweet and mild curry sauce is how you find them in Hong Kong, or in dim sum steamer baskets. It is kinda cheap and a little addictive. In the summer time, you could do as the street food vendors of Hong Kong did—skewer fishballs (in this instance you would use normal white ones), give them a lick of oil, and barbecue them until crisp and golden. A pot of this curry sauce is essential for dunking.

HONG KONG HAWKER-STYLE CURRY FISHBALLS

SERVES 6 AS A SNACK

Place the fishballs in a bowl and fill with just-boiled water. Let soak for 10 minutes to get rid of the excess oil.

Heat the oil in a saucepan and fry the onion with the garlic over medium heat until soft and translucent. Add the flour and stir well so that it evenly coats the onion and garlic. Stir in the curry powder.

Add the water, a little at at time, whisking out any lumps that might develop. Stir in the coconut milk along with the salt and sugar.

Peel the daikon and "roll cut" it: hold the daikon in front of you and make the first cut with your knife at a 45° angle. Roll the vegetable 90° away from you and cut again, repeating until you get to the end. Add this to the pan and stir to combine. Partially cover and simmer gently for 40 minutes—by this time it should be thick and creamy. Add the ketchup and Worcestershire sauce and stir to combine.

Serve as a snack for everyone to help themselves using cocktail picks. Provide napkins.

8 oz package fried fishballs (*see page 129*)

1 tablespoon cooking oil

½ onion, diced

3 garlic cloves, minced

2 tablespoons all-purpose flour

2 heaped tablespoons medium curry powder

2 cups water

⅔ cup coconut milk

hefty pinch of salt

1 teaspoon sugar

7 oz daikon (Asian radish)

1 tablespoon tomato ketchup

dash of Worcestershire sauce

Although it looks deceptively simple with its clear broth and milky white colorings, this fishball noodle soup is full of the flavors of the sea thanks to the dried seafood in the stock. I employ a traditional Vietnamese technique used for making pho by charring the onion, for an extra dimension of flavor.

FISHBALL NOODLE SOUP

SERVES 4

14 oz dried rice vermicelli noodles, or fresh ho fun noodles

1 teaspoon sesame oil (if using fresh noodles)

1 onion, unpeeled, sliced into quarters

2 pints water

2 tablespoons dried anchovies, washed and the heads pinched off

1 tablespoon dried shrimps, washed

1 thin slice of fresh ginger root, peeled

1 star anise

1½ tablespoons lard

4 red Asian shallots, very thinly sliced

16 fishballs (*see page 129*)

1 head of bok choy, sliced through the head into quarters

1 tablespoon fish sauce

1 scallion, green part only, finely sliced into rings

For dried noodles, soak in boiling water following the package instructions, then drain. For fresh ho fun noodles, soak in warm water until the strands have loosened, then simmer for a minute and drain. Run under cold water and toss with 1 teaspoon sesame oil.

Char the onion quarters over the flame of a gas stove or under the broiler until browned and a little blackened on each side. Add to the 2 pints of water in a saucepan, along with the anchovies, shrimp, ginger, and star anise. Simmer gently over low heat for 40 minutes, and then drain through a fine sieve into a new saucepan.

Meanwhile, put the lard into a small saucepan on low heat until it has melted, then add the shallots and turn the heat up to medium. Stir them a couple of times and fry for 3 to 5 minutes, or until they are a light golden brown. Remove the pan from the heat and lift out the shallots with a slotted spoon. Let drain on a dish lined with paper towels. Reserve the lard.

To assemble the dish, add the noodles to each bowl. Reheat the stock on high heat to bring it to a boil, and then add the fishballs and cook in the stock for 3 minutes. Add the bok choy, then turn the heat down to medium and cook for 1 minute. Remove the pan from the heat and stir in the fish sauce. Add a bok choy quarter and 4 fishballs to each bowl. Ladle stock into the bowl so that the noodles are in liquid but not drowning. Garnish with ½ tablespoon of the resesrved lard, a teaspoon of the shallots, and one-quarter of the scallion greens per bowl. Serve immediately.

Known as "yong tau fou," you can use this fish paste to stuff a variety of vegetables—long, mild chiles, halved bell peppers, and okra are popular. I particularly like using eggplant for the silkiness that the eggplant flesh takes on after having been fried and braised. (It may also have something to do with the eggplant being my favorite vegetable.) It's completely customizable, but the scallion gives the fish paste a clean sprightliness, though you could experiment with a flavoring of fresh cilantro, or even seaweed. Traditionally, these are deep-fried and then braised, but I've found that shallow-frying doesn't alter them detrimentally.

FISH PASTE-STUFFED EGGPLANT

SERVES 4 AS A SIDE DISH

Slice the eggplants widthwise into thick slices, about 2 fingers wide. Then slice each section in half, not quite cutting all the way through. Place in a colander, sprinkle with the salt and let stand over a bowl or the sink for 20 minutes.

Meanwhile, mince the scallions. Mix them with the fish paste and set aside.

Mix all the sauce ingredients together, except the cornstarch solution. Prepare a plate with some cornstarch on it for dusting the eggplant.

Rinse the eggplant and dry it with paper towels. Using a tablespoon and your fingers, carefully stuff the fish paste down the slits of each eggplant segment, using as much as the eggplant can take without breaking. Place the eggplant on the plate of cornstarch, turn them so that they are evenly coated, dust off the excess, and transfer to a clean plate. Repeat with the remaining eggplant slices.

Heat the oil in a wok on high heat until shimmering but not smoking. Reduce the heat to medium and cook the eggplant for 4 minutes on each side until browned and starting to soften. Add the sauce mixture, cover, and let braise for 10 minutes.

Stir the cornstarch solution into the wok and simmer gently for a minute to thicken the sauce before serving.

2 slim Asian eggplants or
1 medium eggplant
2 tablespoons salt
2 scallions
7 oz fish paste (*see page 129*)
cornstarch, for dusting
3 tablespoons cooking oil

For the sauce:
1 tablespoon light soy sauce
1½ tablespoons oyster sauce
pinch of sugar
1 tablespoon Shaoxing rice wine
1 cup chicken stock
1 teaspoon cornstarch, mixed with
1 tablespoon cold water

I grew up eating beef tendon, usually in anise-scented noodle soups, so the thought of it doesn't affect me much. It actually makes my mouth water a little. Technically classed as offal, it's not normally seen at the butcher's, but you will find it in the freezer section of the Asian supermarket. It needs to be cooked for a long time for the cartilage to break down to its gelatinous state. It's perfect in these buns—in a classic Cantonese-style sweet and sour sauce, the pickled daikon (Asian radish) and peanuts give a much needed crunch. You can substitute crispy-fried chicken or pork for the beef tendon if you can't find it.

SERVES 4

SWEET and SOUR BEEF TENDON with STEAMED BUNS

1 lb 2 oz beef tendon, defrosted if frozen

2 pints water

1 star anise

1 tablespoon cooking oil

6 garlic cloves, minced

1 teaspoon minced fresh ginger root

1 cup bite-size pineapple chunks
(see page 118)

For the sauce:

3 tablespoons water

1 tablespoon gochujang (see page 16)

2 tablespoons tomato ketchup

2 tablespoons orange juice

1½ tablespoons apple cider vinegar

1 tablespoon Worcestershire sauce

1 tablespoon light soy sauce

2 tablespoons superfine sugar

To serve:

1 package frozen mantou
(steamed bread buns)

1 quantity Pickled Daikon (see opposite)

½ cup peanuts, toasted and ground
to a coarse powder

large bunch of fresh cilantro

Bring a large saucepan of water to a boil. Rinse the beef tendon and blanch in the boiling water for 3 minutes, then drain and rinse again. Return to the saucepan with the 2 pints water and the star anise and simmer on gentle heat, covered, for 3 to 4 hours until tender. Drain the tendon and let cool, then chop into generous bite-size chunks.

While the tendon is cooling, mix all the sauce ingredients together.

Heat the oil in a wok on medium-high heat. Add the garlic and ginger and stir-fry for about 20 seconds, or until just aromatic. Add the pineapple and the sauce mixture, and stir to coat. Let the sauce simmer for about 2 minutes to allow the pineapple to become tender. Return the beef tendon to the pan and toss until it is well coated with the sauce. Let stand on low heat to keep warm.

Steam the mantou buns following the package instructions. Slice each open, stuff with a piece of tendon, a chunk of pineapple, and the Pickled Daikon, and then add a sprinkling of the coarse peanut powder. Garnish each with a sprig of cilantro.

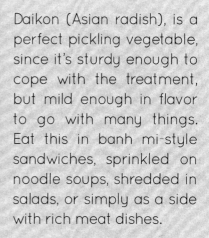

Daikon (Asian radish), is a perfect pickling vegetable, since it's sturdy enough to cope with the treatment, but mild enough in flavor to go with many things. Eat this in banh mi-style sandwiches, sprinkled on noodle soups, shredded in salads, or simply as a side with rich meat dishes.

PICKLED DAIKON

1 lb daikon (Asian radish)
1 large red chile (optional)
1¼ cups warm water
3 tablespoons rice vinegar
⅓ cup white superfine sugar
1 tablespoon fine salt

MAKES

1 LARGE JAR

Peel the daikon and slice into thin disks, then slice in half. Place in a clean, sterilized jar or container.

If using the chile, break it in half and set this on top of the daikon. Mix the warm water with the vinegar, sugar, and salt, and stir until everything is combined. Pour the mixture over the daikon in the jar (the liquid should cover the pickles). Seal with the lid and place in the fridge. Eat after a day—it will last up to a month in the fridge.

To the Chinese, chicken's feet are an everyday sight, common on dim sum and restaurant menus. As a child, I watched fascinated as my grandmother noisily sucked all the skin off the chicken's feet and spat the bones out delicately into a little pile on the table. The point of using chicken's feet is that the skin and cartilage provide a wonderful vehicle for this spicy, finger-licking sauce.

SERVES
6
AS AN APPETIZER
OR SIDE DISH

KOREAN-STYLE CHICKEN'S FEET

1¼ cups vegetable oil, for deep-frying

10½ oz chicken's feet, defrosted if frozen, toenails clipped off with poultry shears, and very thoroughly dried

For the sauce:

1 tablespoon sesame oil

1 small onion, diced

3 garlic cloves, minced

1-inch piece of fresh ginger root, peeled and minced

3 tablespoons gochujang (*see page 16*)

1 tablespoon Korean chili flakes

1¾ cups water

2 tablespoons light soy sauce

1 tablespoon dark soy sauce

1 teaspoon rice vinegar

3 tablespoons sugar

Pour the oil for deep-frying into a wok or large saucepan and heat to 350°F, or until bubbles appear up the sides of a wooden chopstick when inserted into the hot oil. Deep-fry the chicken's feet for 5 to 7 minutes, or until the skin has puffed up and browned slightly. Remove with a slotted spoon and transfer to a wire rack to drain.

Heat the sesame oil in a saucepan on medium heat and fry the onion, garlic, and ginger for 5 minutes, stirring so that they don't brown. Add the gochujang, chili flakes, and the water and stir until thoroughly combined. Add the soy sauces, vinegar, and sugar, followed by the chicken's feet. Braise on low heat, partially covered, for 30 minutes, then turn all the chicken's feet around and braise for another 30 minutes. By this point the sauce should be reduced and sticky; if not, remove the chicken's feet and reduce the sauce down by simmering it until it becomes a sticky glaze, which could take from 10 to 20 minutes. Pour the sauce over the chicken's feet and serve with napkins for messy fingers.

➺ OTHER IDEAS

Steam chicken's feet in black bean sauce, or braise Filipino style in "adobo."

Pork belly and lamb shanks have had a fairly recent resurgence in popularity, but the same can't be said for poor old tripe. With granny's house smelling of tripe boiled with onions being forever etched into the collective memory or simply squeamishness over eating a cow's stomach lining, it's difficult to convince people to give it a chance. The Chinese don't have such hangups about it, and it is prized for its texture. In fact, Asian and Caribbean butchers are the only place I've seen it for sale. This spicy, tangy, in-your-face preparation might go some way to helping you get over your fears.

FIVE-SPICE *and* CHILI OIL COLD TRIPE SALAD

SERVES **4** AS A SNACK

Bring the tripe to a boil in a saucepan of water and boil for 3 minutes, then drain, rinse, and pat dry with paper towels.

Heat the cooking oil in a large saucepan and fry the garlic and ginger on medium heat until fragrant. Add the star anise, cinnamon stick, and five-spice powder, and stir-fry briefly until fragrant. Add the mandarin peel, the tripe, the beef brisket, and the water, and then simmer over very gentle heat for 2 hours. Let cool in the liquor.

Remove the brisket and tripe from the liquor (which can now be discarded) and slice both thinly. Add to a large bowl.

For the dressing, pound the garlic clove with the ginger in a mortar and pestle, and then stir in the chili oil, sesame oil, Sichuan pepper, black vinegar, sugar, and salt. Taste the dressing; it should be salty, sweet, spicy, and tangy in a good balance. Just before serving, stir in the cilantro, and then add the dressing to the brisket and tripe.

5½ oz tripe
1 tablespoon cooking oil
2 garlic cloves
1 slice of fresh ginger root, peeled
2 star anise
1 cinnamon stick
2 teaspoons five-spice powder
(*see page 205 for homemade*)
1 whole dried mandarin peel, soaked in just-boiled water for about 10 minutes until soft, then drained
5½ oz beef brisket
2 cups water

For the dressing:
1 garlic clove, peeled
1 teaspoon peeled and grated fresh ginger root
3 tablespoons chili oil with sediment (*see page 12*)
1 tablespoon sesame oil
1 teaspoon Sichuan peppercorns, toasted and finely ground
1 tablespoon Chinkiang black vinegar
1 teaspoon sugar
½ teaspoon salt
small handful of coarsely chopped fresh cilantro

CHAPTER

PICKLES & PRESERVES

I've always loved anything pickled or preserved, even as a child. As a precocious eight-year-old, I was found in the kitchen smearing butter on soda crackers with my fingers and topping them with half a pitted black olive and a sliver of pickled onion. I still have a habit of eating cornichons straight from the jar, fishing the capers out of the brine, and often my favorite part of a burger is the gherkin. I love sour things, though my teeth hate me for it.

Most cultures and cuisines have a method of preserving food, from air-drying or smoking, to brining and salting. The Asian cultures are no different, and Asian supermarkets hold a vast treasure trove of pickled goods. I'm often found wandering the aisles, studying the limited English writing on the sides. Most often, I hoard serving-sized vacuum packets of various vegetables, sometimes with "Nutrition for students" bafflingly printed on them. I can only assume it is in reference to their longevity. These are great as rice or congee toppings (*see page 58*). This is by no means an exhaustive list, but simply a guide to what I've found most readily available.

A lot of the preserved vegetables you'll find are mustard greens. They are sturdy vegetables, making them the ideal candidate for pickling. You can buy them in various guises, from their soft leaves to the vivid, angry-red bulbs of their stems. They can be found in liquid or dry-packed in salt, canned, or vacuum packed. Most, if not all, pickled and preserved vegetables should be washed beforehand to remove some of the excess salt and brine.

PICKLED MUSTARD GREEN

This is your standard head of mustard green, usually halved, in brine and vacuum packed. Some may have a lone red chile floating in there with them. These are good all-rounders for soups and stir-fried dishes.

SICHUAN ZHA CAI

If you have looked around a Chinese wet market, you will have seen this bulbous livid-red thing in open-topped barrels. In supermarkets, they are most often found canned or shredded in a vacuum pack. This is the mustard-green root. It is salted and pressed before fermenting with chile paste, and is a little like kimchi (*see page 143*). You can stir-fry this with shredded pork, fold it into noodles, or use it on top of tofu (bean curd) or congee (*see page 58*) for a spicier pickle kick.

SICHUAN YA CAI

This consists of mustard-green leaves only, chopped up and left to ferment with salt, and they're essential in dishes like dan dan noodles and dry-fried green beans. I've only ever found these in vacuum-packed foil bags.

MUI CHOY

This is another form of mustard green but instead of being pickled in brine, it's dried and packed in salt, sometimes with the addition of sugar. Because of the preservation process, you must rinse these thoroughly, otherwise your dish can become gritty. It is most often used in braised meat dishes.

OLIVE VEGETABLE

From southern China and a Teochew local delicacy, olive vegetable is a dark and murky paste that comes in a jar. It's actually the leaves of mustard greens mashed and preserved with black olive flesh and oil; sometimes you'll find olive stones in the jar. It's dramatically dark and great for stir-frying with. Just hold off on the salt—it's plenty salty enough as it is.

TIANJIN PRESERVED VEGETABLE

This is one of my favorite pickled vegetables. From the Tianjin metropolis of northern China, this is made with Chinese cabbage (Chinese leaf or Napa cabbage). The pieces of cabbage are sun-dried, then combined with salt and garlic before being placed in an earthenware pot to ferment. You usually buy it in clay pots, and it lasts forever in the cupboard. A quick rinse before using it is essential, because it's very salty.

KIMCHI

Often called the national dish of Korea, almost any vegetable can be given the kimchi treatment, "kimchi" referring to the spicing and fermentation process (*see pages 48 and 143*).

DRIED LILY BUDS/FLOWERS

Also called golden needles, but not to be confused with golden needle mushrooms, these are the unopened flowers of day lilies. Sold in packages, they look like brown woody stems and need to be rehydrated in just-boiled water before using them. Some recipes call for them to be tied in knots before use to prevent them from breaking up. If you have nimble fingers, then go for it, otherwise it's not that critical if you don't knot them. The buds taste slightly floral and woody, but not overwhelming, and suit stir-fries and braises.

TSUKEMONO

This is the collective term for Japanese pickles. Most Japanese pickles are for eating with meals as accompaniments rather than for cooking with. Japanese sections will often have a variety of brightly colored pickles, ranging from yellow to purple, and red to green. I use umeboshi plums most often, as a snack or as a filling for onigiri (rice balls).

SOUR BAMBOO SHOOTS

Available in a jar preserved in brine or vacuum packed, sour bamboo shoots are mostly used in Thai cooking. They have a very distinctive aroma that will linger if you leave any open and hanging around. They are best suited to soups and curries—see page 174.

CENTURY EGGS

These are ready-to-eat duck eggs that have been buried in alkaline clay for some time so that when peeled the whites of the egg are black and transparent, and the yolks green-gray. Most people baulk when they see these, because they are certainly dramatic looking, but they are also mellow in flavor. Expensive premium century eggs have a yolk that is still runny. Chop the eggs up into congee (see page 58) or soups, or stir-fry them with ground chicken, basil, and chile. They are also great in salads (see page 176).

SALTED EGGS

These are duck eggs that have been preserved by submerging them in brine or by packing a damp charcoal paste around them, often sold with the charcoal residue still in place. This preserving process renders the egg white very white and liquid, while the egg yolk takes on a firmer, slightly fudgy consistency. They are not immediately ready to eat; once cooked, they impart a great eggy saltiness and a sandy texture. The Chinese use salted egg yolks in not only savory but sweet dishes, notably mooncakes eaten at Mid-autumn Festival; those made with the yolk are the most expensive, and the yolk is said to symbolize the moon. To use the yolk, crack the egg and discard the egg white. Otherwise, boil the egg as you would do a normal egg.

WHITE & RED FERMENTED TOFU
(BEAN CURD)

Often called "Chinese cheese," white fermented tofu is cured in brine to create funky, silky smooth cubes that are sold in jars. It's usually eaten as a condiment or as a rice or congee topping (see page 58) straight from the jar, but it's also stir-fried with vegetables (see page 183). It's available flavored with sesame or chili oil, as well as plain. The red variety, available in jars or cans, is tofu that has been fermented in red rice yeast and is much stronger in taste. It's rarely eaten as it is but is used for marinating and braising meat.

Dill is an herb I associate with Scandinavian cuisine and, in turn, smoked salmon, mackerel, and gravadlax. But it's used all over the world, from the Mediterranean, through the Middle East and even in China. This broth-based soup is light, fragrant, and flavorsome, with the hearty tang of the mustard green at the forefront.

VIETNAMESE PICKLED MUSTARD GREEN & MEATBALL SOUP

SERVES 4 AS A LIGHT LUNCH

¾ lb ground pork

1-inch piece of fresh ginger root, peeled and minced

1 garlic clove, minced

scant handful of fresh cilantro, finely chopped

1 tablespoon oyster sauce

½ teaspoon salt

pinch of ground white pepper

1 teaspoon cornstarch

2 pints chicken stock

1 red bird's-eye chile, split in half (optional)

1 pickled mustard green (*see page 160*), drained and soaked in cold water for 30 minutes

pinch of sugar

2 large tomatoes, cut into 8 wedges

1 small bunch of dill, cut into 1-inch segments

1 to 2 tablespoons fish sauce

Combine the pork with the ginger, garlic, cilantro, oyster sauce, salt, white pepper, and cornstarch in a bowl, mixing well with your hands so the mixture holds together well. Don't overmix it, otherwise the meatballs will be tough. Form into golf ball-sized balls.

Heat the stock in a saucepan over high heat until simmering, then lower the heat to stop it from boiling. Add the halved chile, if using. Chop the mustard green into bite-size pieces, discarding the tough stalk, drop it into the stock, and simmer for 10 minutes. Add the meatballs, sugar, tomatoes, and two-thirds of the dill and simmer for another 15 minutes on gentle heat. Add 1 tablespoon of fish sauce and taste, then add more if needed.

Add the rest of the dill, then serve.

This is the kind of home comfort meal I love most, one that I make when I'm eating alone and I don't have any guests to entertain, which seems silly since it's so quick and tasty. It's what I imagine my younger self might have lived off had I gone to university. The noodle sauce is spicy and tangy from the preserved vegetable; creamy and satisfying from the egg. The key to fluffy, soft eggs is for the egg mixture to hit hot, plentiful oil to allow it to bubble and fluff up.

SICHUAN PRESERVED VEGETABLE, EGG *and* TOMATO NOODLES

SERVES
2

Bring a saucepan of water to a boil to cook the noodles following the package instructions.

Meanwhile, heat 1 tablespoon of the cooking oil in a wok over medium heat. Add the garlic, preserved vegetable, and the whites of the scallion and stir-fry for 2 minutes, then add the tomatoes and stir-fry for 1 to 2 minutes, or until the tomatoes are starting to soften and release their juices. Add the water, sugar, ketchup, rice wine, and soy sauce. Simmer for a minute, then transfer to a bowl and wipe the wok clean.

Drain the noodles well and place in a large warmed dish.

Add the remaining ¼ cup of cooking oil to the wok. Give it a good swirl and heat it over medium–high heat until it's just below smoking.

Add the beaten eggs to the oil; they will puff up and sizzle. Stir the egg with chopsticks until it has scrambled a little, then return the cooked tomato mixture to the wok along with the greens of the scallion and stir and fold everything a couple of times. If the sauce is looking too watery, add the cornstarch solution. If it's sticking to the wok, add a dash more water.

Remove the pan from the heat and pour the contents over the noodles, drizzling the chili oil on top before serving.

7 oz bundle of dried wide, flat wheat noodles

⅓ **cup** cooking oil, divided

2 garlic cloves, minced

knob of Sichuan zha cai preserved vegetable (*see page 162*), soaked in water for 20 minutes, then rinsed and finely chopped

1 scallion, white and green parts separated, minced

2 **large** ripe tomatoes, coarsely chopped

3 **tablespoons** water

pinch of sugar

squeeze of tomato ketchup

1 **teaspoon** Shaoxing rice wine

1 **teaspoon** light soy sauce

2 free-range eggs, beaten with a pinch of salt

1 **teaspoon** cornstarch, mixed with 1 **tablespoon** cold water (optional)

1 **teaspoon** chili oil

Chinese sausage (lap cheong) works well in this dish thanks to its sweetness contrasting with the intensely savory olive vegetable, which is like a Chinese tapenade *(see page 162)* that speckles everything dramatically with black. Beware of olive pits.

OLIVE VEGETABLE-FRIED RICE *with* CHINESE SAUSAGE

SERVES 4

3 tablespoons cooking oil, divided

2 Chinese sausages, diced

dash of Shaoxing rice wine

1-inch piece of fresh ginger root, peeled and minced

2 garlic cloves, minced

1 carrot, peeled and diced

1 celery stalk, peeled and diced

handful of sugar snap peas, chopped into thirds

2¼ cups cooled cooked rice

1 tablespoon light soy sauce

3 tablespoons olive vegetable *(see page 162)*

1 scallion, minced

4 free-range eggs

sriracha *(see page 109 for homemade, or use ready-made)*, to serve

Add 2 tablespoons of the cooking oil to a wok over high heart. Just before it starts smoking, add the diced Chinese sausage and stir-fry for 1 to 2 minutes to release some of the oils. Splash the rice wine in and stir until it has evaporated. Add the ginger and garlic and stir-fry for 30 seconds, then add the carrot and celery, followed by the sugar snap peas. Stir-fry for 1 minute to soften the vegetables.

Over high heat, add the rice by crumbling it through your fingers to make sure that the grains are separated. Let the rice fry until the grains near the center of the wok start jumping, then start moving the rice around. Drizzle the rice with the soy sauce and stir-fry again. Then add the olive vegetable, moving the rice around constantly so that it distributes evenly. Stir in the scallion and set the wok aside.

Heat the remaining tablespoon of cooking oil in a nonstick skillet over medium heat and fry all 4 eggs for 3 minutes, then cover and fry for 2 minutes longer to ensure that the yolks are still runny but the whites have set.

To serve, spoon each portion of rice into a bowl and upend onto a plate to create a dome shape. Drape a fried egg on top and serve with sriracha for people to help themselves.

➥ OTHER IDEAS

Braise cubes of butternut squash with olive vegetable made into a sauce with a little stock, or serve with congee *(see page 58)*.

There are two different types of mui choy, sweet and salty, and this recipe uses both. You can tell which is which on the plastic package, since the salted version contains only salt, while the sweet contains salt and sugar. This type of preservation makes the mustard green almost herbal in flavor; slightly but not unpleasantly medicinal. This is a classic Hakka dish—the sweetness of the pork-belly fat mellows it all out a little, and makes you return to it with your rice bowl repeatedly. This type of mustard green tends to be very gritty, so don't skimp on the preparation process.

MUI CHOY PORK BELLY

SERVES
6
WITH
OTHER
DISHES

Rub the slices of pork belly with the dark soy sauce and the five-spice and set aside.

Rinse the mui choy well. Bring a large saucepan of water to a boil over high heat, plunge the mui choy into the water, and blanch for 3 minutes, stirring a few times. Drain, rinse with cold water, and let soak in cold water for 20 minutes. Drain well, then cut the leaves into ½-inch pieces and the stems into ¼-inch pieces.

Heat the cooking oil in a wok on medium heat and fry the slices of pork belly, skin-side down first, then on both sides, for a minute. Transfer to a heatproof bowl, arranging the slices skin-side down. Stir-fry the mui choy in the remaining fat in the wok until some of the residual moisture has dried out, then add the ginger, garlic, and star anise and stir-fry for a minute. Remove and place on top of the pork-belly slices.

In a large measuring cup or pitcher, mix the hot water with the rice wine, light soy sauce, oyster sauce, and rock sugar, stirring until the sugar has dissolved. Pour this over the mustard greens in the bowl. Cover the bowl with foil or an appropriate lid and steam in a pan with a steamer insert or on a wire rack in a wok on medium heat for 2 hours. Top off the water if it's running dry.

To serve, place a large plate over the bowl and very carefully turn the bowl over onto the plate so that the pork belly sits on top of the mustard greens. Serve with plenty of steamed white rice and other vegetable side dishes.

1 lb 9 oz pork belly, skin on, sliced into slices as thick as 2 fingers

1 tablespoon dark soy sauce

pinch of five-spice powder
(*see page 205 for homemade*)

5½ oz sweet mui choy
(*see page 162*)

5½ oz salty mui choy
(*see page 162*)

1 tablespoon cooking oil

3 slices of fresh ginger root, about ¾ inch thick, peeled and finely chopped

6 garlic cloves, minced

2 star anise

1¼ cups hot water

1 tablespoon Shaoxing rice wine

1 tablespoon light soy sauce

1 tablespoon oyster sauce

1½ teaspoons Chinese rock sugar or white superfine sugar

➥ OTHER IDEAS
You can also mix the mui choy into ground meat and steam it, like a Chinese meatloaf.

I don't know when mu shu pork became so popular in American Chinese restaurants, but the same can't really be said for ones in the UK (in my experience). I hadn't heard of it before I bought a package of dried lily buds on a whim, but my research told me that it was a classic ingredient of the dish, so in it went. This meal has been a staple for a while now; when I'm feeling overindulged or I'm just looking for a lighter meal, it comes to my rescue. You might find the lack of pancakes somewhat perplexing, but I find the crunch of the Little Gem leaves far superior. After all, if you want pancakes, roast duck is the only thing to stuff them with.

MU SHU PORK

Combine the light soy sauce, water, rice wine, and cornstarch in a bowl. Add the pork, stir well to coat, and then let marinate while you prepare the other ingredients.

Drain the lily buds and tie each into a knot (this is to prevent them from breaking up during stir-frying). Heat 1 tablespoon of the cooking oil in a wok over high heat and swirl it around until just below smoking. Pour the beaten eggs in and let set as a round disk. You may need to scramble the center and put the lid on to allow more heat to reach the rest. Once the egg has set, remove it from the wok and set it aside. Let cool for 5 minutes, then roll it up and slice it thinly.

Wipe the wok clean and heat the remaining tablespoon of oil over medium heat until it is shimmering. Add the onion, garlic, and ginger and stir-fry for 1 minute until fragrant and the onion is softening. Increase the heat to maximum and immediately add the pork, cabbage, bean sprouts, carrot, mushroom, and the lily buds. Stir-fry constantly on the highest heat for 3 to 5 minutes, or until the pork is cooked and the vegetables are starting to soften. Add the slices of omelet and stir to combine.

Remove the pan from the heat, drizzle in the sesame oil, and garnish with the scallion. Place in a serving dish with the Little Gem leaf cups for people to spoon the pork mixture into.

1 tablespoon light soy sauce

1 tablespoon water

1 teaspoon Shaoxing rice wine

1 tablespoon cornflour

3½ oz boneless pork shoulder or loin, cut into thin strips

1 oz dried lily buds (see page 162), soaked in just-boiled water for 20 minutes

2 tablespoons cooking oil, divided

2 free-range eggs, beaten with a pinch of salt

1 small onion, sliced into half-moons

2 garlic cloves, minced

1 teaspoon peeled and grated fresh ginger root

3½ oz Savoy or sweetheart cabbage, leaves separated and thinly sliced

1 cup bean sprouts

1 carrot, peeled and julienned

1 dried cloud ear or wood ear mushroom, soaked in just-boiled water for 15 minutes, then drained and julienned

1 teaspoon sesame oil

1 scallion, thinly sliced diagonally

1 head of Little Gem lettuce, leaves separated and washed, to serve

The joy of these buns is in their fried bottoms. Steamed buns can at times be a bit too pillowy and sweet; in frying these, they become crunchy with a fluffy top. In my eagerness to eat them, I invariably burn my mouth and dribble pork juices down my chin. At least it's never dull.

PORK PRESERVED VEGETABLE BUNS

MAKES **12**

For the dough:
1¾ cups bread flour, plus extra for dusting
¾ cup all-purpose flour
1 teaspoon fast-action dried yeast
2½ tablespoons sugar
1 scant teaspoon salt
2 tablespoons cooking oil
¾ cup water

For the filling:
3 leaves of Chinese cabbage (Chinese leaf or Napa cabbage)
1 tablespoon fine salt
1¾ oz Tianjin preserved vegetable (*see page 162*)
1-inch slice of fresh ginger root, peeled
1 scallion
10 oz fatty ground pork (fat is important here, to keep the insides juicy)
2 teaspoons light soy sauce
2 teaspoons sesame oil
1 teaspoon sugar
pinch of ground white pepper
1 teaspoon cornstarch
1 tablespoon cooking oil, plus a little extra for frying a sample of the filling to check the seasoning

For the dipping sauce:
1 tablespoon Chinkiang black vinegar
½ tablespoon water
pinch of sugar
1 tablespoon chili oil

Combine all the ingredients for the dough, except the water, in a mixing bowl. Add the water, a little at a time, until you get a soft dough. Knead by hand on a lightly floured work surface, or use an electric stand mixer with a dough hook, for 5 minutes, or until smooth. Return it to the bowl, cover with plastic wrap, and let rise in a warm place for an hour.

Meanwhile, make the filling. Slice the cabbage leaves in half lengthwise and chop finely. Add to a colander and sprinkle with the fine salt. Let stand over a bowl or the sink for 20 minutes for all the water to drain out.

Meanwhile, add the preserved vegetable to a large bowl of water to rinse some of the salt out. Let this stand for 20 minutes too.

Chop the ginger and scallion very finely and add to the pork with the soy sauce, sesame oil, sugar, pepper, and cornstarch. Mix with chopsticks in one direction until all is well amalgamated.

Rinse the cabbage and drain well, then add to the pork mixture. Rinse the preserved vegetable and chop coarsely, then also add to the pork. Mix together well. Fry a teaspoonful of the mixture in a little cooking oil in a nonstick skillet and taste to check the seasoning.

Tip the risen dough onto a floured work surface. Knead lightly a couple of times, then roll into a sausage shape and cut into 12 even pieces.

Press down on each piece of dough to form into a rough circle.

Roll the circle out to the size of your palm. It's preferable to have the middle a little thicker than the edges.

Add about a tablespoon of filling to each circle.

Then start gathering in the sides of the dough.

You should end up with a neatly sealed bun. Place the buns on a floured plate while you make the rest.

Twist until you have sealed the bun. Give the seal a pinch to ensure it's properly closed.

To cook, heat the oil in the nonstick skillet and fry the buns flat-side down. When the bottoms are browned, add a few splashes of water, cover, and let steam. Repeat a couple of times for about 8 minutes until cooked through. While the buns are steaming, mix the dipping sauce ingredients together in a serving bowl. Serve the buns hot with the dipping sauce.

Shaved thinly, sour bamboo shoots have a very particular smell of a musky pickled-ness that, although not unpleasant, does have a tendency to linger, and they need soaking to remove some of their saltiness. This simple Thai red curry is fragrant with basil, but is also sweeter than usual to counteract the acidity of the bamboo shoots.

SOUR BAMBOO SHOOT CURRY

SERVES
2

Soak the sour bamboo shoots in a large bowl of water for 30 minutes to get rid of some of the saltiness, then drain.

Heat the oil in a saucepan or wok over medium heat. Add the coconut milk and bring to a simmer, then stir in the curry paste and simmer for 5 minutes. Add the sour bamboo shoots and simmer for 20 minutes, then slide in the hake fillets and lime leaves. Simmer gently for another 5 minutes (or more, if your fish is thicker) until the fish is cooked through. Taste before adding the fish sauce, since the shoots can still be very salty. Add the sugar to balance, remove from the heat, and add the Thai basil leaves. Squeeze the lime wedge over the dish, stir, and serve immediately with rice.

7 oz sour bamboo shoots (*see page 163*)

1 tablespoon cooking oil

14 fl oz can coconut milk

2 tablespoons Thai red curry paste

2 hake fillets

5 kaffir lime leaves

1 tablespoon fish sauce

1 teaspoon jaggery (palm sugar)

handful of Thai basil leaves

wedge of lime, for squeezing

Your friends, and even you, will probably baulk at the look of this dish. Admittedly, transparent black egg whites and greenish-gray yolks aren't exactly appealing. But century eggs are really very mild in flavor and actually very pretty with this garnish. At least they'll be a talking point.

CENTURY EGG SALAD

SERVES 4 TO 6
AS AN APPETIZER OR SIDE

2 century eggs (*see page 163*)
1 large red chile
1 large green chile
1 scallion
2 tablespoons soy sauce
½ tablespoon Chinkiang black vinegar
½ teaspoon superfine sugar
a few fresh cilantro leaves

Tap the eggs all over with a teaspoon and peel the shell off carefully (submerging them in water makes the shell come away more easily). Halve each of the eggs, then place on a serving plate, cut-side up.

Seed the red and green chiles and chop them very finely with the scallion. Scatter the egg halves with this mixture.

Mix the soy sauce, vinegar, and sugar together, stir until the sugar has dissolved, and then drizzle the mixture over the egg halves. Garnish with the cilantro leaves.

These century eggs are fried until they're crisp on the outside, with a slightly gooey center. The star of the show here, though, is the chicken, so it's worth making this even if you can't find the blackened eggs. Sweet, salty, a little spicy and sour, the basil leaves give the dish fragrance, and it's quick to make.

THAI FRIED CENTURY EGGS *with* CHICKEN

SERVES 2 WITH OTHER DISHES

2 tablespoons cooking oil, or more if needed

large handful of Thai basil (Italian basil works too), leaves plucked off of the stems and divided equally into 2 piles

2 century eggs (*see page 163*), shelled (*see method on page 176*) and quartered

2 garlic cloves, minced

1 bird's-eye chile, coarsely chopped

1 boneless, skinless chicken breast, roughly ground by hand

½ teaspoon superfine sugar

1 tablespoon fish sauce

1 tablespoon oyster sauce

1 tablespoon light soy sauce

¼ lime

Pour the oil into a wok and set over medium heat. Fry half of the basil leaves for about 45 seconds, or until crisp. Transfer to a plate lined with a piece of paper towel.

Next, fry the egg pieces, turning them so that they are cooked on all sides, for at least a minute each side until they are crisp. Remove and set them aside on a plate.

Place the wok back over medium heat, add the garlic and chile along with a drizzle more oil if it's a little dry. Stir-fry for 2 minutes, and then add the ground chicken, sugar, fish sauce, oyster sauce, and soy sauce. Continue to stir-fry until the chicken is completely cooked, which shouldn't take more than 5 minutes in total.

Finally, stir in the rest of the Thai basil leaves until they are slightly wilted, and then transfer the chicken mixture to a plate. Arrange the fried century eggs around it, and scatter with the fried basil leaves. Squeeze juice from the lime quarter over the dish and serve with steamed rice and a couple of other dishes.

Oh wibbly, wobbly joy. This dish celebrates all three types of egg: preserved, salted, and fresh. The preserved and salted eggs add flavor; the fresh eggs give it body. Special care should be taken when steaming to avoid overcooking, because that would be a sad thing indeed. You're aiming for a just-set, wobbliness, like a panna cotta. Eaten with some plain rice it is the ultimate comfort food. And you can customize the flavorings as you see fit; maybe fried ground pork flavored with ginger, or add chopped marinated uncooked shrimp halfway through the steaming process to finish off cooking in the egg.

STEAMED EGG CUSTARD *with* CENTURY *and* SALTED EGGS

SERVES 2 WITH OTHER DISHES

Set up a metal or bamboo steamer ready to go.

Crack the fresh eggs into a bowl and beat with a fork. Add hot water (which should be a comfortable temperature when you stick a finger in it) using each of the eggshells—you want a ratio of 1:1.5 egg to water, so use each half once and 2 halves once more. Beat again. Pour through a sieve (the sieve gets rid of the foam of the egg, which would make a bubbly surface on the finished dish) into a baking dish small enough that the mixture rises to at least 2 inches deep.

Shell the century egg (*see method on page 176*) and cut into dice. Then crack the salted egg, discard the egg white, and chop the yolk in half. Scatter these into the egg mixture.

Cover with plastic wrap and set inside the steamer. Steam for about 8 minutes over high heat, checking constantly. You want wobble but not liquid.

Meanwhile, slice the green part of the scallion diagonally. Mix the soy sauce with the sesame oil and water.

When the egg custard has set, remove it from the heat. Pour the soy sauce mixture evenly over it, and then garnish it with the scallion greens. Serve immediately.

4 free-range fresh (chickens') eggs
1 century egg (*see page 163*)
1 salted egg (*see page 163*)
1 scallion, green part only
1 tablespoon light soy sauce
1 teaspoon sesame oil
½ tablespoon water

This really is a dish to dive into with your hands, possibly wearing a bib. The luxurious combination of the salted egg yolks and butter flavors the evaporated milk (don't use condensed—there's quite an important difference) with the delicate aroma of the curry leaves. Rip the heads off the shrimp, suck the head juices out, lick your fingers, and repeat. You may need to wash afterward.

SALTED EGG BUTTER SHRIMP

SERVES

2

1 large red chile

1 small red chile

3 salted egg yolks (*see page 163*)

3 tablespoons cooking oil

8 raw jumbo shrimp in their shells

2 tablespoons butter

2 garlic cloves, lightly crushed but leaving them whole

10 fresh curry leaves

3 shallots, finely sliced

⅓ cup evaporated milk

½ teaspoon superfine sugar

Chop the large chile coarsely, and cut a slit in the small chile but leave it whole. Add the egg yolks to a small heatproof bowl and steam in a metal or bamboo steamer over high heat for 10 minutes, or until cooked. Let cool a little, then mash with the back of a spoon.

Heat the cooking oil in a wok on high heat until it shimmers. Add the shrimp and stir-fry for 1 minute so that they're half-cooked. Remove and drain on paper towels. Drain the rest of the oil out of the wok, reserving 1 tablespoon.

Add the butter and garlic cloves to the wok and stir-fry for 2 to 3 minutes over medium heat until fragrant. Add the curry leaves and red chiles, followed by the shallots, and stir-fry to combine for 1 minute. Then stir in the salted egg yolks and add the evaporated milk and sugar. Simmer for 5 minutes.

Return the shrimp to the wok, coating them with the sauce and moving them around until they're fully pink and cooked, which should only take a couple of minutes. Dish out onto a serving plate and serve with plenty of napkins.

You'll often find fermented white tofu (bean curd) flavored with sesame oil or chile, and you can use either kind in this recipe instead of plain.

SUGAR SNAP PEAS, SCALLOPS & BABY CORN *with* WHITE FERMENTED TOFU

SERVES
2

Heat the cooking oil in a wok on high heat until just below smoking and sear the scallops on each side for about 30 seconds, or until they have a golden brown crust. Remove from the wok and set aside.

Add the baby corn to the wok and stir-fry for a minute on high heat, then add the garlic, sugar snap peas or asparagus, tofu, soy sauce, and rice wine with the water. Stir-fry constantly for about 1 minute, or until the vegetables are almost tender. Return the scallops to the wok, carefully turn them over a few times, and then remove the pan from the heat. Serve with the scallion placed on top, with some steamed rice on the side.

1 tablespoon cooking oil

8 large shelled scallops, preferably with roes attached

3½ oz baby corn, cut in half, then in half again lengthwise

1 garlic clove, minced

5½ oz sugar snap peas, or green asparagus, woody tips snapped off and cut into 3-inch pieces

2 cubes of white fermented tofu (bean curd) (*see page 163*), mashed with a fork

1 teaspoon light soy sauce

1 teaspoon Shaoxing rice wine

3 tablespoons water

1 scallion, julienned

This is a Cantonese classic, eaten on hot rice with a drizzle of roasting juices. The red fermented tofu *(see page 163)* is crucial for the right flavor, and is indeed great to marinate or stew any meat for a deeper, more intensely savory flavor.

CHINESE ROAST PORK BELLY

If your piece of pork belly has bones, remove these so that the slab sits as level as possible. If the skin hasn't been scored, do so with a very sharp knife but only cut the skin. Do not cut through the fat to the flesh.

Place the piece of pork belly on a rack in the sink and pour a full kettle of just-boiled water carefully, slowly, and evenly over the skin of the belly in the sink. Let stand to drain and dry.

Mix the fermented tofu with the five-spice, 1½ teaspoons of salt, the sugar, and garlic. Dry the piece of pork belly with paper towels and set on a plate, skin-side down. Score the flesh about half the depth of the meat into wide strips (so perhaps 3 times), then rub the marinade all over the pork belly meat and into the cuts. Turn it back over, dry off the skin, and rub it with 1 tablespoon of salt. Let marinate in the fridge, uncovered, for a minimum of 4 hours or overnight.

Take the pork belly out of the fridge about an hour before cooking so that it can come up to room temperature, and wipe the salt off of the skin. Preheat the oven to 425°F, rub the skin with a little cooking oil, and place the pork on a rack in a roasting pan, skin-side down. Pour enough boiling water into the roasting pan to cover the bottom of it, but not so that it touches the pork. Roast for 25 minutes, then turn it over and roast it for another 30 minutes. (If your piece of pork belly is bigger than 2¼ lb, roast for 20 minutes per pound of the total weight, plus 20 minutes.)

Remove the pork from the oven and let rest for 15 minutes. If the skin isn't crisp or hasn't puffed up much, place under a hot broiler for a few minutes (and watch it like a hawk) until it has puffed.

To serve, carve the pork into thick slices or bite-size pieces. Fan out on a plate for everyone to help themselves with a small bowl of Homemade Sriracha *(see page 109)* for dipping.

1¾ lb piece of boneless pork belly with skin

2 cubes of red fermented tofu (bean curd) *(see page 163)*, mashed with a fork

½ teaspoon five-spice powder *(see page 205 for homemade)*

salt

1 teaspoon sugar

2 garlic cloves, very finely grated

cooking oil, for rubbing

Homemade Sriracha *(see page 109)*, to serve

CHAPTER

SPICES & DRIED VEGETABLES

SPICES & DRIED VEGETABLES

A huge part of Asian supermarkets is taken up by the dried foods. The Chinese probably use more dried goods than the other Asian cuisines; their earthy, dried mushrooms are used not only to flavor stews, but in salads, and to provide additional texture, while five-spice powder and star anise spices are essential flavorings for certain dishes, usually involving meat. You may notice after your wanderings around the supermarket that I haven't included any traditional Chinese medicinal herbs; that's mainly because getting into that area would be a whole new book. And it's better to stick to things that taste nice...

(1, 2, 3, 4 & 5) STAR ANISE, CASSIA BARK, CINNAMON, CUMIN, FENNEL & CURRY SPICES

These are the spices used mostly in braising or marinating meats. The southern parts of China use a lot of star anise (1), cassia bark (2), and cinnamon (3), while the northern parts such as Xinjiang use cumin (4) and fennel (5) more.

FIVE-SPICE POWDER

A common spice mix, usually consisting of star anise, cloves, cinnamon, Sichuan peppercorns, and fennel seeds, and used in braising. It is sold in most supermarkets (check the label; some brands include salt), or make your own (*see page 205*).

(6) CHILES & SICHUAN PEPPERCORNS

There are different types of dried chili, but most common are the bell-shaped, romantically named "heaven-facing chiles," and the long thin chiles. Sichuan peppercorns (6) are a joy themselves for their unique ability to make your mouth go a little numb.

(7 & 8) MUSHROOMS

Shiitake (7) are the most commonly available type of dried mushroom, but you will also come across cloud ear and wood ear mushrooms (8).

SEAWEED

The Japanese use wakame seaweed, sold dried, mostly in salads and soups. Kombu is sold as large sheets for you to cut up and use to flavor stocks like dashi (*see page 209*). Nori comes in sheets, which are paper thin and used as wraps for sushi and onigiri (rice balls), but can also be toasted until crisp, crumbled into flakes, and used as a seasoning or garnish. Purple seaweed, usually sold dried in disks, is used solely for Chinese soups.

(9, 10 & 11) DRIED TOFU
(BEAN CURD)

This is made by skimming the surface of soy milk in production to lift off the top layer of skin (much like what you may have seen on top of custard). This is then dried into a variety of shapes and formats to suit different preparations. Tofu bamboo (9) are sticks of dried skin gathered up, tofu skins (10) (called yuba in Japanese) are flat, dried sheets which can sometimes be wrinkled up a little, while tofu knots (11) are, as you might suspect, tofu skin tied into knots. Dried sheets of tofu are normally used for sweet dessert soups while tofu sticks, which are a little sturdier, are reserved for stews.

Tofu knots are often added to soups and stews for additional texture, and they also retain the juices within the knot, creating a flavorsome mouthful. Tofu bamboo is commonly used in salads. In all cases, dried tofu needs to be rehydrated before use.

DRIED FLOWERS & FRUITS

Dried chrysanthemum flowers are used to make tea (*see page 210*), and dried goji berries can flavor dishes or form a flavoring in their own right (*see page 210*).

GINKGO NUTS

Ginkgo nuts are usually sold in cans or vacuum packed. Eaten most commonly at special occasions, such as Chinese New Year or weddings, they are often served with congee or desserts, and are said to have health benefits.

RED AZUKI BEANS

Sold as dried beans, ready-cooked in cans, or mashed and sweetened into a paste, red azuki beans are used most frequently in desserts.

This is, undoubtedly, kind of a gnarly one. Fish HEAD? You mean, I have to eat a head? Well, yes. Sorry about that. But fish do have heads, and heads happen to be really quite delicious. Especially that nugget of cheek just under the eyes—it's soft and smooth, silky and tender. If you have any really brave friends, they might be up for eating the actual eye. Alternatively, you can make this with fish fillets—you'll just need firm, white fish, preferably with skin to hold it together. You might recognize a lot of the spices in this dish from Indian cooking, since Malaysian cuisine is an intriguing mixture of Chinese and Indian influences.

MALAYSIAN FISH HEAD CURRY

SERVES
2

1 fish head—ask your fish dealer for this; red snapper, hake, and cod are all good, but avoid oily fish like salmon

1 tablespoon sea salt flakes

1 tablespoon cooking oil

1 tablespoon tomato paste

14 fl oz can coconut milk

½ cup water

1 teaspoon sugar

8 okra, halved widthways

3 tomatoes, quartered

½ teaspoon salt

½ lime, for squeezing

leaves from 2 sprigs of fresh cilantro, to garnish

For the spice paste:

1 onion, coarsely chopped

5 garlic cloves, coarsely chopped

1-inch piece of fresh ginger root, peeled and coarsely chopped

1-inch piece of fresh galangal root, peeled and coarsely chopped

½ tablespoon coriander seeds, toasted and ground

1 teaspoon chili powder, or to taste

1 teaspoon ground cumin

½ teaspoon ground turmeric

1 teaspoon fennel seeds, toasted and ground

1 tablespoon cooking oil

Rub the fish head with the sea salt flakes and set aside.

Blend all the ingredients for the spice paste together in a blender to a fine paste.

Heat the cooking oil in a wok over medium heat until it is shimmering and fluid. Add the spice blend, turn the heat down low, and fry for 10 minutes, stirring often. Add the tomato paste, coconut milk, water, and sugar, and then stir well so that everything is combined. Simmer on medium heat with the lid off for 15 minutes. Add the okra and simmer for another 5 minutes.

Rinse the salt from the fish head. Add it to the wok so that it is submerged in the sauce. Set the tomatoes around the fish head, cover, and simmer gently for 15 minutes (less if using fillets), turning the fish head once during this time. Season with the salt and spoon out into a deep serving dish. Squeeze the lime juice evenly over the curry, garnish with the cilantro leaves, and serve with rice.

20 **dried** heaven-facing (bell-shaped) chiles

3 **slices** of fresh ginger root, peeled

2 **tablespoons** Sichuan peppercorns

2½ **pints** chicken stock

1 **teaspoon** salt

6 **oz** firm tofu (bean curd), cut into chunks

10½ **oz** skinless pollock fillet, cut into chunks

2 scallions, diagonally sliced

SICHUAN FISH *and* TOFU HOTPOT

SERVES 4 WITH OTHER DISHES

Sichuan peppercorns have the glorious ability to make your mouth tingle and become numb when you eat them. They have a slightly metallic, citrus tang to them, and after a big Sichuanese meal I often find myself craving more. This is probably the spiciest recipe in the book. It looks the part, with a vast sea of chiles bobbing around in the broth, but you're not supposed to eat them; they're there to flavor, not to annihilate. The chiles are charmingly named "heaven facing," since, apparently, that's what they look like they're doing.

Add the chiles, ginger, and Sichuan peppercorns to the stock in a saucepan and simmer, partially covered, for a good 40 minutes. Add the salt and the tofu chunks for the last 10 minutes of the cooking time.

Finally, add the fish to the broth and remove from the heat. Let stand, covered, for 10 to 15 minutes to cook the fish through. Garnish with the scallions and serve. Instruct your guests to fish out the tofu and the pollock, spooning minimal broth onto lots of steamed white rice as they go.

Katsu curry is often regarded as the junk food of Japan and, since we're breading and deep-frying meat before smothering it in sauce, I'm not really in a position to refute that. But although it is the antithesis of Zenlike sushi and miso soup, it is still a wonderful thing in its own right; the curry sauce is mild and sweet, fragrant, and silky against the crisp meat. It is unchallenging, warming, and everything you want from comfort food.

CHICKEN KATSU CURRY

SERVES 4

2 boneless, skinless, chicken breasts, sliced in half lengthwise

¼ cup all-purpose flour, seasoned generously with salt and pepper

1 free-range egg, beaten

2 handfuls of panko bread crumbs

1 cup cooking oil

For the sauce:

1 tablespoon cooking oil

1 onion, diced

4 garlic cloves, minced

2 carrots, peeled and coarsely chopped

1½ tablespoons medium curry powder

1 heaped tablespoon all-purpose flour

2½ cups chicken stock

2 dessert apples

1 tablespoon light soy sauce

1 teaspoon superfine sugar

Place the chicken breast halves between 2 sheets of plastic wrap and lightly hammer them with a rolling pin to thin them out a little to a uniform thickness. Set aside and repeat with the rest of the chicken.

Heat the cooking oil for the sauce in a large saucepan and gently fry the onion over very low heat for 10 minutes, or until soft and translucent. Add the garlic and fry for 3 minutes, then stir in the carrots. Add the curry powder and the flour and stir well to combine. Then gradually whisk in the stock to avoid lumps. Peel, core, and grate the apples into the saucepan and finally add the soy sauce and sugar. Let the mixture simmer gently on low heat for 30 minutes.

Preheat the oven to 225°F. Place the seasoned flour on a plate and the beaten egg on another plate (or in a shallow bowl). Place the panko bread crumbs on a third plate. Pour the cooking oil into a wok or saucepan large enough to accommodate the chicken breasts and heat to 350°F, or until bubbles appear up the sides of a wooden chopstick when inserted into the hot oil. Then dip the chicken, one piece at a time, first in the flour, then in the egg, and finally in the bread crumbs before slipping it into the hot oil. Fry for 4 minutes on each side, turning the chicken over if is not completely submerged in the oil. Transfer to a rack set on a baking pan and place in the oven while you fry the rest of the chicken.

Cut each piece of chicken into 3 slices and serve with the sauce and steamed rice. You can pass the curry sauce through a sieve on to the rice if you like, but actually I like all the bits of vegetable, so I rarely bother with the sieve.

➤ OTHER IDEAS

Use the curry sauce as a sauce for french fries for an exotic alternative to tomato ketchup.

Spiced nuts aren't a new or unusual idea, but I particularly like these for the buildup of that numbing feeling as you're chowing down. These cashews are the perfect beer snack; spicy, salty, and incredibly addictive.

SERVES
2
AS A
SNACK

SICHUAN PEPPERCORN CASHEWS

1 tablespoon cooking oil

½ teaspoon fine sea salt

1 teaspoon dried chili flakes

1 teaspoon Sichuan peppercorns, toasted and finely ground

1⅓ cups unsalted raw cashews

Preheat the oven to 325°F. Line a baking pan with nonstick parchment paper and set aside.

Combine the oil with the sea salt, chili flakes, and half the ground Sichuan peppercorns in a bowl. Add the nuts and toss well to coat in the mixture. Spread them out in a single layer on the lined baking pan and roast for 15 minutes, turning a couple of times so that they cook evenly.

Remove from the oven and let cool for 5 minutes, then place in a bowl and sprinkle with the remaining Sichuan pepper.

This curry is classic winter food, though often eaten for breakfast; beef cooked until soft and almost collapsing in a spiced and thick sauce. I love the inclusion of both potato and daikon (Asian radish), an alternating bite between creamy stodge and the crisper, cleaner "radish." The Vietnamese still maintain culinary traditions derived from French colonization, and this is reflected in the baguette that is often served with it for dipping in the sauce.

BO KHO
(VIETNAMESE BEEF CURRY)

SERVES 4

If using the annatto seeds, heat the cooking oil in a skillet, add the seeds, and cook over medium heat for 5 minutes, then remove from the heat and set aside until cool. Sieve the annatto seeds out of the oil.

Toss the diced beef with the flour and fry in the annatto oil (or plain cooking oil) in a large saucepan until browned. Add the onion, garlic, ginger, and lemon grass, and stir to combine. Fry for another 3 minutes before adding the star anise, curry powder, coriander, fennel, five-spice powder, and cinnamon stick. Mix well and fry for an additional 5 minutes on low heat.

Add the canned tomatoes, plus a can of water. Simmer gently over the lowest heat, uncovered, for 2 hours, stirring every so often. If it's looking dry, add a little more water. Then add the carrots, daikon, and potato, and simmer for about 40 minutes.

Add the fish sauce, stir to combine, and taste the mixture. Add more fish sauce if it needs it. Serve with a hunk of baguette or some rice to soak up the sauce.

2 **tablespoons** cooking oil

2 **tablespoons** annatto seeds (optional)

1 **lb 9 oz** beef shin (shank), or any other slow-cooking beef, cut into bite-size pieces

¼ **cup** all-purpose flour

1 onion, coarsely chopped

5 garlic cloves, squashed with the side of a knife

2-**inch** piece of fresh ginger root, peeled and minced

2 lemon grass stalks, chopped in half

3 star anise

1 **tablespoon** medium curry powder

1 **teaspoon** ground coriander

1 **teaspoon** fennel seeds, toasted and ground

1 **teaspoon** five-spice powder (*see page 205 for homemade*)

1 cinnamon stick

14 **oz** can chopped tomatoes

2 carrots, peeled and roll cut (*for method, see page 153*)

1 small daikon (Asian radish), peeled and roll cut (*for method, see page 153*)

4 long white potatoes, washed and chopped into 4

1 **tablespoon** fish sauce, or to taste

This is a minimal-effort dish, but one that brings a high reward. Especially popular with children, the cola reduces down to a sticky and addictive glaze. If you use other chicken portions, it will be inferior; you really need the finger-licking quality that wings bring to it. I'm not saying it's good for you, but once in a while...

COLA CHICKEN WINGS

1¾ **lb** chicken wings

2 **tablespoons** dark soy sauce

3 garlic cloves

2 scallions

2 **tablespoons** vegetable oil

3 **slices** of fresh ginger root, peeled

1 star anise

2 **tablespoons** light soy sauce

1 **can** of cola (not diet or flavored)

drizzle of sesame oil

Split the wings at the joint (one wing makes 2 pieces, the "flat" and the "drum"). Place in a bowl and rub with the dark soy sauce. Let marinate for a few minutes and, while doing so, crush the garlic and separate the white and green parts of the scallions, chopping the whites coarsely and slicing the greens diagonally.

Heat the vegetable oil in the wok over medium heat and brown the chicken pieces well. Remove and set aside. Stir-fry the garlic, ginger, and whites of the scallions with the star anise. Return the chicken wing pieces to the wok, stir to coat, and add the light soy sauce. Open the can of cola and pour into the wok. Bring to a boil, then let it simmer for 20 minutes. The liquid may not quite cover the chicken pieces, in which case turn the pieces over and simmer for another 20 minutes. By this point the sauce should have reduced to become thick and glossy. If not, simmer it for a little longer.

To serve, arrange on a platter and garnish with the scallion greens. Drizzle with the sesame oil and serve with steamed white rice and a vegetable side dish or two (*see page 84*).

This is the kind of dish that is made for winter. The star anise works beautifully with beef, and you'll find that your whole house smells aromatic and a little spicy, while you tap your foot, impatiently waiting for it to finish cooking. Cuts of beef that work particularly well are those with some fat on them or some connective tissue in them, so that it all breaks down with the slow cooking into a delicious, lip-smearing, beefy hug. I sometimes use half ox cheek and half beef tendon (see page 156 for cooking instructions) for a little textural contrast.

RED-BRAISED OX CHEEK

SERVES **4** WITH OTHER DISHES

Bring a saucepan of water to a boil. Add the ox cheek pieces and blanch them for 2 to 3 minutes. Drain and rinse the ox cheek pieces, and rinse the pan out. This step gets rid of the scum that clouds the broth. Place the ox cheek pieces in a clay pot (*see page 11*) or fit them snugly into the rinsed-out saucepan.

Heat the cooking oil in a wok and stir-fry the chili bean paste with the ginger, garlic, and scallion whites. Add the yellow bean paste and rice wine, then the star anise and the stock or water. Bring to a boil and add to the ox cheek. Cover, and braise very slowly over low heat for 3 to 4 hours, or until the ox cheek is tender. Top off with a little water (or stock if it didn't all fit) if it's looking dry.

Serve, garnished with the scallion greens, on rice or on noodles.

1 lb ox cheek or other beef for slow cooking, cut into bite-size pieces

2 tablespoons cooking oil

2 tablespoons chili bean paste (*see page 16*)

¾ oz fresh ginger root, peeled and thinly sliced, then pounded with the side of a knife

3 garlic cloves, slightly crushed

2 scallions, white parts only, chopped into 3-inch pieces, green parts reserved and sliced

1 tablespoon yellow bean paste (*see page 16*)

2 tablespoons Shaoxing rice wine

1 star anise

2 cups beef stock or water

My favorite restaurant in London, Silk Road, makes these lamb skewers with chunks of pure lamb fat interspersed with the meat; they become crispy and juicy once grilled over intense heat. As soon as they put the plate down on the table, hands come out of nowhere grabbing at them. I have, on many occasions, tried to solicit some sort of recipe out of the guys there, but to no avail. This is as close as I've got—it's something of a different beast, since it works with a wet marinade rather than a dry spice rub, but it is pretty great nonetheless. Lamb fat optional.

SERVES 4

XINJIANG LAMB SKEWERS

1 lb 7 oz boneless lamb shoulder
2 tablespoons cumin seeds
1 teaspoon Sichuan peppercorns
2-inch piece of fresh ginger root, peeled and minced
4 fat garlic cloves, minced
3 teaspoons ground cumin
pinch of salt
3 tablespoons chili bean paste (*see page 16*)
4 scallions

Chop your lamb shoulder into cubes and put into a bowl.

Toast the cumin seeds in a dry skillet on medium heat for a couple of minutes until you can smell their aroma, shaking the pan often to stop them from burning. Let cool, then grind in a mortar and pestle, or a spice or coffee grinder if you have one. Do the same with the Sichuan peppercorns.

Add both spices to the lamb along with the ginger, garlic, cumin, and salt and mix well, then add the chili bean paste. Cut the scallions into pieces 1 inch long, add them to the lamb, and mix together. Cover the bowl with plastic wrap and let marinate in the fridge for a few hours or overnight. Meanwhile, if you don't have metal skewers, presoak some wooden ones in water for a good 30 minutes (but even so, beware of them catching fire; metal are better).

Take the lamb out of the fridge a couple of hours before cooking so that it comes up to room temperature. Thread the lamb onto your skewers, alternating with the scallion. Cook on a hot barbecue, or a smoking hot ridged grill pan on the stove, for a few minutes each side so that they are charred and cooked through but not burned. Serve with a cooling salad.

Quail might well be my favorite (edible) bird. Their tiny bodies don't take long at all to cook and, provided you use high heat, you are well rewarded with crisp skin and juicy meat that you can eat a little pink. The pleasure may also be to do with feeling like a giant, ripping off those teeny-weeny drumsticks.

FIVE-SPICED QUAIL

SERVES 4 WITH OTHER DISHES

4 oven-ready quails
2 garlic cloves, peeled
½ teaspoon salt
1 tablespoon liquid honey
2 teaspoons five-spice powder
(*see below for homemade*)
1 teaspoon dark soy sauce
½ teaspoon Sichuan peppercorns, toasted and finely ground
2 tablespoons cooking oil, divided
1 lime, cut into wedges

Spatchcock your quails. Do this by first placing a quail breast-side down on your cutting board and removing any trussing bands that might be holding its legs together. Then cut lengthwise along the center of the underside of the quail with a sharp knife, turn the quail breast-side up, and push the breastbone down with your palm to flatten it. Place them in a shallow dish and set aside.

Using a mortar and pestle, coarsely pound the garlic with the salt. Add the honey, five-spice, soy sauce, Sichuan pepper, and 1 tablespoon of the oil and mix together well. Rub this mixture all over the quails, cover the dish with plastic wrap, and let marinate in the fridge overnight.

Take the quails out of the fridge a couple of hours before cooking to come to room temperature. Preheat the oven to 400°F. Heat the remaining tablespoon of oil in a heavy cast-iron or nonstick skillet over medium heat. Add the quails (if you can fit them all in the same pan) skin-side down and fry them for 5 minutes, pressing down on them with a spatula all the while so they cook evenly and the skin becomes crisp. Once bronzed, flip them over, and then transfer to a roasting pan and roast for 10 minutes. Serve with lime wedges.

MAKES
1 SMALL JAR

You will notice that there are six spices in my five-spice. I'm a rule breaker. These spices are all available to buy whole and cheaply at the Asian supermarket.

DIY FIVE-SPICE POWDER

Toast all the spices in a dry skillet on medium heat for 3 to 4 minutes, or until they are aromatic, shaking the pan often. Let cool, then grind in a spice or coffee grinder. Keep in an airtight container.

25 star anise **(about ¾ oz)**
3 tablespoons fennel seeds
¾ oz cassia bark
¼ cup Sichuan peppercorns
1½ tablespoons black peppercorns
1 teaspoon cloves

This is a comforting type of dish. The oyster sauce, chicken flavors, and mushroom juice meld together to make an addictive, slightly sweet sauce that you will almost abandon the chicken for, just to spoon it over white rice. The mushrooms soak up the sauce too, so that every time you bite into one, a great gush of juices is released into your mouth. Truly, the chicken plays second fiddle here. Don't forget the rock sugar; I've made this recipe so many times, wondering what was missing, and that was it.

SERVES 2

BRAISED CHICKEN, BROCCOLI and SHIITAKE MUSHROOMS

1 tablespoon Shaoxing rice wine

1 tablespoon light soy sauce

½ teaspoon ground white pepper

3 skinless chicken thighs on the bone, each chopped into 3 pieces through the bone—you can ask your butcher to do this, or carefully do it yourself using a sharp cleaver

2 tablespoons cooking oil

5 thin slices of fresh ginger root, peeled

5 garlic cloves, minced

10 dried shiitake mushrooms, soaked in cold water overnight then drained

1½ tablespoons oyster sauce

⅔ cup water

2 teaspoons or 1 small lump of Chinese rock sugar

1 scallion

6 broccoli florets

1 teaspoon cornstarch, mixed with **2 tablespoons** cold water

Mix the rice wine, soy sauce, and white pepper together in a bowl. Add the chicken thigh pieces, turn to coat well, and cover with plastic wrap. Let marinate in the fridge for at least an hour (overnight is ideal), but the dish won't suffer too much if it's a shorter period of time.

Heat the oil in a wok on high heat until it is shimmering but not smoking. Stir-fry the ginger slices and garlic until fragrant, then add the chicken plus its marinade and stir-fry until it has lost a little of its rawness and taken on some color.

Cut off the mushroom stems and add the mushrooms to the wok, along with the oyster sauce, water, and the rock sugar and stir to combine. Cover and let braise on low heat for 30 to 45 minutes. Or, you can decant the mixture to a clay pot (see page 11) to braise, freeing up your wok to cook vegetables or another dish.

Slice the white of the scallion into 3-inch pieces, then cut them in half lengthwise. Add to the pan or pot along with the broccoli florets, cover, and cook for another 5 minutes, still on low heat. Test the broccoli for tenderness. If it's still a little firm, give it a couple more minutes.

Add the cornstarch solution to the pan or pot, stirring it in well. When the sauce thickens and becomes glossy (usually within about a minute), the dish is ready. Carefully invert onto a plate so that the chicken and mushroom mixture lies on top of the broccoli. Slice the greens of the scallion finely and scatter on top to serve.

5 **dried** cloud ear or wood ear mushrooms, soaked in just-boiled water for 15 minutes, then drained

1 **large** carrot, peeled and julienned

$1/3$ **cup** blanched shelled fava beans or peas

3 tofu bamboo sticks (*see page 189*), soaked in just-boiled water for 30 minutes

1 **large** red chile, sliced into thin rings (optional)

1 scallion, sliced into 3-inch pieces and very thinly sliced lengthwise

1 **tablespoon** rice vinegar

1 **teaspoon** salt

2 **teaspoons** sesame oil

½ **teaspoon** sugar

CLOUD EAR FUNGUS *and* TOFU BAMBOO SALAD

SERVES 4 AS A SIDE

This salad is a great combination of textures: the cloud ear mushrooms are crunchy and a little slithery, while the tofu bamboo is smooth, silky, and slightly chewy. It's a pretty plate of spring colors, and you can add or substitute other vegetables like bell peppers, blanched broccoli, or roasted cauliflower into the mixture.

Chop the mushrooms into quite large pieces but discard the tough core. Add to a bowl with the carrot and the fava beans or peas.

Drain and squeeze the tofu bamboo gently, then rip coarsely into 3. Add to the mushrooms. Throw in the sliced chile, if using, and the scallion.

Whisk the rice vinegar with the salt, sesame oil, and sugar. Drizzle the mixture evenly over the vegetables and toss to coat. Serve immediately.

This is an incredibly traditional Chinese soup, made using disks of purple seaweed called zi cai (or zhee choy in Cantonese). I haven't found any other use for this type of seaweed other than in soups, and when suspended in liquid it has a throat-sweeping, silky texture as it goes down. I find it very soothing. If you can't find clams, replace them with mussels, thinly sliced white fish, soft silken tofu (bean curd), or chicken.

SERVES

PURPLE SEAWEED EGG DROP SOUP

3 cups chicken stock

1 teaspoon peeled and minced fresh ginger root

1 tablespoon Shaoxing rice wine

4 small chunks of loofah gourd (*see page 82*) (optional)

¼ oz dried purple seaweed, soaked in cold water for 10 minutes

14 oz live clams, scrubbed clean

pinch of ground white pepper

1 free-range egg, beaten with

2 tablespoons light soy sauce

1 scallion, green parts only, shredded

Place the stock in a saucepan with the ginger, rice wine, and the loofah gourd, if using, then bring to a gentle simmer and let cook for 3 minutes.

Drain the purple seaweed and add it to the saucepan along with the clams and white pepper. Cover and let simmer for another 3 to 5 minutes, or until the clams have opened. Discard any that do not open.

Remove the pan from the heat and, while stirring the soup gently in one direction, pour the beaten egg into it so that the strands are suspended in the liquid. Top with the scallion greens and serve with an additional bowl for the discarded clam shells.

piece of dried kombu (*see page 188*), about 6¼ x 8 inches

2 pints water

handful of dried bonito flakes

Place the kombu and water in a large saucepan and let stand for 10 minutes. Bring to a boil and, just as it boils, remove from the heat. Add the bonito flakes and let stand for 10 to 15 minutes, then strain through a fine sieve to use.

MAKES

ABOUT 2 PINTS

HOW TO MAKE DASHI

Dashi is the backbone of Japanese cuisine. You can buy it in powdered form, but it is so easy to make that I prefer to do so myself. From here you can mix it with white miso paste to make miso soup, and use it for simmering liquids and noodle broths. It is also often used in dipping sauces.

There are a few different types of dashi. One kind involves shiitake mushrooms, called shiitake dashi, but there is also niboshi dashi, made by pinching the heads off of dried baby sardines and using them to flavor the stock. But the most commonly used is kombu dashi, made with katsuaboshi, which are dried bonito flakes (shavings from a dried, smoked skipjack tuna). You can buy them in big resealable bags.

↠OTHER IDEAS
Dried bonito flakes are often placed on top of noodles, noodle soups, or savory pancakes called okonomiyaki. The steam from the food makes them look like they're waving or dancing.

When I was a kid, my mother used to boil a load of dried chrysanthemum flowers in water to make a tea, and sweetened it with Chinese rock sugar. I was told that this tea is particularly good for you when you've eaten too much fried food, and can also help clear your complexion. Whether or not that is true, it's still a delicious drink, floral, mildly herbal, and perfect during hot summer months.

CHRYSANTHEMUM TEA

1¾ oz dried chrysanthemum flowers
1½ quarts water
1 oz Chinese rock sugar

Rinse the dried flowers in a sieve and add to the water in a large saucepan over high heat. Bring to a boil, reduce the heat to low, and simmer for 5 minutes.

Remove the pan from the heat and add the rock sugar. Stir to dissolve, and then let cool. Strain through a fine sieve and drink either cold or at room temperature.

Goji berries, sold dried, plump up to become soft and sweet in this herbal tea. You can enjoy this hot or cold.

GOJI BERRY LEMON TEA

SERVES 1

1 tablespoon dried goji berries
1 black tea or Earl Grey tea bag, or tea of your choice
1 slice of lemon
honey, to taste

Wash the dried goji berries and place in a mug. Add the tea bag of your choice and pour boiling water over it. Let steep for 1 minute, and then use a teaspoon to squeeze the remaining water out of the tea bag and discard it.

Let stand for 5 minutes to allow the goji berries to plump up. Add the slice of lemon, honey, to taste, and serve.

For a while, goji berries were hailed as a superfood, and started appearing in the mainstream. But the Asians have been enjoying them for years, steeped in teas, in dessert soups, or in savory dishes. They are sweet and inoffensive, a welcome splash of color to what could otherwise be a dreary plate. This dish has no danger of appearing dreary—there's a lovely ceremony to bringing a whole fish to the table for people to pick at with chopsticks.

STEAMED BREAM with GOJI BERRIES

SERVES 4 WITH OTHER DISHES OR 2 AS A MAIN

Preheat the oven to 400°F. Place a large sheet of foil in a roasting pan, and then line the bottom of the pan with nonstick parchment paper. Scatter half the matchsticks of ginger onto the parchment paper, and then set the fish on top. Cut 2 slits at right angles to the spine of the fish through the flesh and scatter the goji berries on top. Drizzle the water around it. Gather up the sides of the foil, rolling and crimping to make a tight seal so that no steam can escape. Place in the oven to steam for 13 to 15 minutes (13 for a small/medium bream or sea bass, 15 for a larger fish). The flesh should come away from the bones easily.

Remove the fish from the foil and carefully transfer to a serving plate, taking the goji berries with it but discarding the ginger and pouring off any liquid that has accumulated. Scatter the fish with the scallions and the remaining ginger.

Meanwhile, heat the oil in a small saucepan on medium heat to just below smoking. Remove from the heat to cool for 20 seconds. Then, very carefully tilting the oil away from you, pour in the light soy sauce, dark soy sauce, sesame oil, and sugar. It may splatter, so stand back. Swirl and stir to combine, then pour over the fish.

Serve with other vegetable sides (see page 84) and some plain steamed rice.

2-inch piece of fresh ginger root, scraped clean of skin and sliced into very thin matchsticks

1 whole sea bream or sea bass, gutted and scaled

2 tablespoons dried goji berries

3 tablespoons water

2 scallions, sliced into 4-inch pieces and julienned

2 tablespoons cooking oil

2 tablespoons light soy sauce

1 teaspoon dark soy sauce

1 teaspoon sesame oil

1 teaspoon superfine sugar

The Asians use red azuki beans, either mashed into a paste or whole, as a dessert ingredient, for soups, ice cream, and fillings. When I was growing up, I loved the ice pops you could buy in the stores. These ice pops were flavored with nutty, creamy, sweetened red beans that gave them a dramatic reddish-purple color, but you could also get olive-green mashed green mung-bean versions. You can buy sweetened red bean paste at the Asian supermarket, but I prefer to make it myself so that I can control the texture and the sweetness.

RED BEAN ICE POPS

MAKES **4** TO **6** DEPENDING ON YOUR MOLD SIZE

Open the can of beans and drain the water out of it, or drain the cooked dried beans. Reserve 3 heaped tablespoons of the beans. Add the rest of the beans to a saucepan along with the coconut milk, sugar, and salt and simmer, uncovered, on very low heat for 15 minutes.

Remove from the heat and let cool for 10 minutes. Using a hand-held stick blender, blend until smooth, and then pass the mixture through a fine sieve. Stir the reserved beans into the mixture, then spoon into 4 to 6 ice-pop molds. Freeze for at least 4 hours. To serve, dip each frozen mold in hot water for 10 seconds to release the ice pops.

14 oz can azuki beans in water or **1 cup dried** azuki beans, soaked in cold water overnight then drained and simmered in 2 pints fresh water for 1 hour, or until soft

1½ cups coconut milk

⅓ cup sugar

pinch of salt

Black sesame ice cream is dramatic; gray-black in color, it often draws startled gasps from dinner guests who haven't seen it before. I like adding berries to a bowl of this ice cream, but served with the sesame honeycomb, this is a flavor explosion. The honeycomb is also good eaten just as it is, with coffee.

BLACK SESAME ICE CREAM with BLACK and WHITE SESAME HONEYCOMB

SERVES 4

Beat the egg yolks and sugar in a bowl until creamy.

Toast the black sesame seeds in a dry nonstick skillet on medium heat for 1 to 2 minutes, or until they become fragrant. Do not let them burn. Let cool, and then grind them finely using a spice or coffee grinder if you have one, or using a mortar and pestle.

Add the ground sesame seeds to the milk in a large saucepan, then add the cream. Heat until it comes to just under boiling (about 3 minutes). Watch it like a hawk and then remove the pan from the heat.

Add the vanilla and let it infuse for 30 minutes in a cool place. Add a few spoonfuls of the milk mixture to the egg mixture and stir well. Keep adding the milk mixture until all is incorporated, then return the pan to low heat, stirring and heating until it has thickened and resembles custard. Do not let it boil.

Strain the sesame seeds out through a sieve and put the mixture in the fridge to cool thoroughly before churning/freezing in an ice-cream maker, following the manufacturer's directions. Alternatively, you can add the mixture to a freezerproof container, seal, and place it in the freezer for a couple of hours until almost frozen. Then, use a hand-held stick blender (or transfer to a blender) to break down the ice crystals. You will need to repeat the process 3 to 4 times until the ice cream is frozen in order to avoid any lumps of ice.

To make the black and white sesame honeycomb, toast the sesame seeds in a dry skillet over medium heat for about 5 minutes, or until browned and fragrant but not burned, stirring often. Set aside. Line a large baking pan with nonstick parchment paper, allowing the paper to overlap the sides generously.

Heat the sugar and light corn syrup in a large, heavy saucepan (you'll see why you need a large one later) over low heat, stirring occasionally, until the sugar has melted into liquid form. This will take about 10 minutes. Turn the heat up to medium and let it bubble for 7 minutes, or until it turns a deep amber color—but not any darker than that. Remove from the heat immediately and add the toasted sesame seeds and vanilla extract, stirring well. Then add the baking soda and stir quickly. At this point the mixture will bubble and froth; spoon it quickly onto the lined baking pan and set aside. Get your saucepan into hot water as quickly as you can, before the caramel sets onto it. If needed, refill the pan with boiling water to melt the sugar residue.

Let the honeycomb cool for 2 hours, and then break it into pieces. It tends to break randomly, so if you want neat pieces, cut it with a serrated knife, using a sawing motion. Store in an airtight container and eat within a couple of days. Or, coat each piece entirely in melted chocolate and it will keep pretty much indefinitely.

For the ice cream

2 free-range egg yolks

½ cup superfine sugar

½ cup black sesame seeds

1½ cup cups lowfat milk

1 cup heavy whipping cream

1 teaspoon vanilla extract

For the honeycomb

¼ cup white sesame seeds

¼ cup black sesame seeds

1 cup superfine sugar

⅓ cup light corn syrup

½ teaspoon vanilla extract

2 teaspoons baking soda

It might seem odd to have a soup for dessert, but it's very common in Cantonese cuisine, and this is a particularly classic one. The tofu (bean curd) becomes soft and willowy, flavoring the soup to resemble soy milk. This, like many soups, has a basis simply of water sweetened with Chinese rock sugar (which the Chinese believe is good for the lungs), called tong sui in Cantonese. I can't say this will be to everyone's taste, but it's certainly a change from Western-style desserts. If this is a bridge too far for you, you can also make savory soups and stews with the tofu skin.

CANTONESE BEAN CURD SKIN DESSERT SOUP

SERVES 4

2 pints water

2½ tablespoons pearl barley, washed

2 sheets of dried tofu skin (*see page 189*), broken into pieces with your fingers and soaked in cold water for 10 minutes

3 pandan leaves, tied in a knot

2¼ oz Chinese rock sugar

3 tablespoons ginkgo nuts (*see page 189*), from a vacuum pack or a can

Bring the water to a boil in a large saucepan with the pearl barley, tofu skin pieces, and the pandan leaves. Simmer for 30 minutes.

Remove the pandan leaves and discard. Add the rock sugar and ginkgo nuts and let simmer for another 10 minutes. Serve warm or cold.

Dim sum can often consist of steamer upon steamer of intricately pleated dumplings, where the skill of a deft touch and a lightness of hand is needed to make them. These meatballs, however, are far more forgiving and easy to make. Here, the tofu bamboo protects the meatball from sticking to the plate, but it also soaks up all the juices released during cooking.

STEAMED BEEF BALL DIM SUM with TOFU BAMBOO

SERVES 4 AS AN APPETIZER OR SNACK

Dice the lard into very small pieces and add to a bowl along with the ground beef. Then add all the remaining ingredients, except the tofu bamboo and Worcestershire sauce. Mix everything together with your hands, folding the meat over and squeezing gently for about 5 minutes, or until it becomes well combined and sticky. Let stand for 30 minutes to marinate.

Mix again for another 5 minutes, then gather it up in your hands, giving it a squeeze, and then slap it hard back into the bowl or onto a clean work surface. Repeat 10 times. This gives the characteristic "bouncy" texture once steamed.

To cook, line a plate with a lip with the tofu bamboo straightened out into sheets and place in a metal or bamboo steamer. Arrange the steamer in a wok half-filled with boiling water (but so deep that it touches the steamer). Roll the beef into 10 balls, each around 1½ inches in diameter, and place on the plate. Cover, and let steam in the wok on high heat for 10 minutes. At this stage you can split one in half to check whether it's cooked through; if not, let steam for another 3 minutes.

Drizzle with Worcestershire sauce before serving.

2½ tablespoons lard
7 oz ground beef
1 teaspoon grated orange zest
1½ tablespoons oyster sauce
½ teaspoon ground black pepper
1 teaspoon peeled and grated fresh ginger root
small handful of fresh cilantro, very finely chopped
½ teaspoon baking soda
1 tablespoon cornstarch
½ teaspoon salt
1 tablespoon sugar
1½ oz drained canned water chestnuts, coarsely chopped into small pieces (to yield about ⅓ cup)
1 scallion, very finely sliced
4 tofu bamboo sticks (see page 189), soaked in just-boiled water for 15 minutes
2 tablespoons Worcestershire sauce, to serve

INDEX

ACKNOWLEDGMENTS

Thanks firstly go to my awe-inspiring agent, Diana Beaumont. Thank you to Mitchell Beazley and the team for putting this together—Yasia, Stephanie, Sybella—you're all great. Thank you for the belief in my idea, thank you for your patience and hard work. Thank you David, Tab, Annie, and Abi for making it look just how I wanted it to, and more.

I'd like to thank my parents, Hazel and Peter, for having the good sense to meld their genes together. Credit too goes to them for bringing me up to be such a greedy person, always looking forward to my next meal, and always planning my circumstances around something delicious. It is a special skill honed through the privilege of being a Mabbott.

To my enduring friends and housemates, Emily, Luke and Chris. For all the washing up, for stuffing yourselves silly, and eating all that weird stuff I put upon you. I made you trim the nails from chickens' feet. I made you gut chickens. You put tripe in your mouths unwillingly. I am grateful.

Big thanks also to EuWen, Cherry, Melon & Donald, Nicola and Adam for helping me out in my time of need. I'd also like to thank Naz and Jane for being awesome creative gurus, and to Joe, for the wonderfully conditional support. Thank you, Macca, for the killer fruit facts, and to James, for the opportunity.

Finally, a huge thanks to Stevie for being my sounding board, my strategist, my jar of self-belief, my guinea pig, my wine pusher, my cheerleader. I'd be a jibbering wreck if it weren't for you. I'll never force coconut crème pâtissière on you again.